Career Killers/
Career Builders

JOHN CROSSMAN

Endorsements

"John Crossman is a leading authority and expert on inspiring students to build strong career paths. His impactful speech entitled 'Career Killers' is enjoyed by students and motivates them to truly consider their future and take the necessary steps to grow into successful professionals."

—Caryn Beck-Dudley, Dean of the Leavey
School of Business at Santa Clara University

"John is one of the most impactful speakers and mentors to our students I have had. He is a pleasure to work with. He doesn't tell students what they want to hear, he tells them what they need to hear. It is that type of honesty and straightforwardness that makes him an amazing asset to our program and why we constantly ask him back to speak."

—Joshua A. Harris, PhD, CRE, CAIA, Director,
Dr. P. Phillips Institute for Research and Education
in Real Estate at the University of Central Florida

"John is a tremendous resource for students interested in real estate, especially in the retail sector. He understands what it takes to be successful and is willing to share his insights. No need to experience a 'career killer' moment firsthand when you can learn in advance from John. He is truly vested in seeing people succeed."

—William G. Hardin III, PhD, FRICS, Professor of
Finance and Real Estate at Florida International University

"John has spoken to over three thousand of my students through the years. He is highly regarded each year by my students."

—Betsy Goodman, JCPenney Director
at the Warrington College of Business

"John has spoken to countless students in our college and university. His passion for their success, combined with his unique ability to connect with them on a personal level, has inspired and motivated our students to reach their fullest potential."

—Michael D. Hartline, PhD, Dean,
College of Business at Florida State University

"A highly successful businessman, respected by his peers, John Crossman has not forgotten his beginnings. Consequently, he has devoted much time, energy, and financial support toward helping students succeed in business. His book, *Career Killers/Career Builders*, based on a popular series of lectures in business schools, is essential for those who aspire and those who want to learn from a master."

—Luder Whitlock, Retired President
of Reformed Theological Seminary

"John Crossman speaks from experience! In business, he has clearly demonstrated that integrity, honesty, and careful preparation are the essential building blocks of a successful career. In *Career Killers/Career Builders*, his straightforward and down-to-earth approach has made this book a must-read for anyone who wants to get and keep a job!"

—Jerry Ross, President of National Entrepreneur Center

"John Crossman has been dedicated to enlightening and mentoring others by creating multiple venues, such as his book *Career Killers/Career Builders*, to assist young men and women in their professional growth."

—Mike Foley, Former Chairman, ICSC Foundation

"John's book provides straightforward advice on how to start and nurture a career."

—Peter Linneman, Albert Sussman Professor of
Real Estate, Finance, and Public Policy at the
Wharton School of the University of Pennsylvania

"John has been working to inspire and mentor students for years. In *Career Killers/Career Builders*, he lays a strong foundation to help students not just dream about their future but take the right steps to get there."

—Danny Wuerffel, Former NFL Player and Heisman Trophy Winner

"John Crossman is extremely passionate about positively impacting the lives of students while they are in school and continuing to support them after graduation. I had the opportunity to personally observe John's significant efforts on behalf of students while serving with him on the ICSC Foundation Board of Directors."

—Peter Eisenberg, Clark Street Real Estate

"John Crossman is a successful business executive who understands the critical need to prepare the next generation of business leaders by sharing his knowledge. Fortunately for us, he is also very good at translating his experiences into entertaining, motivational formats that make it easy to learn from him. This book contains insights that will be relevant to anyone who rises to a position in management. I look forward to sharing it with my students."

—David Paradice, Harbert Eminent Scholar
in Business Analytics at Auburn University

"John is an inspiration to many students."

—Terry Prather, Retired President of Sea World

"John Crossman is an inspirational leader and mentor to young adults beginning their careers in business and real estate. Every student and young professional should take the time to contemplate the lessons discussed in *Career Killers/ Career Builders*. It can take a lifetime to build a reputation, but only one mistake to destroy it. Read it, practice it, live by it!"

—Juan Martinez

"In sharing lessons learned over his impressive career in the real estate industry, John Crossman delivers a series of keen insights peppered with humorous anecdotes and wise counsel. *Career Killers/Career Builders* reveals a valuable roadmap for students of all ages who aspire to professional and personal success."

—Jim Spaeth, University of North Carolina Professor

"For many years, John Crossman has been passionate about helping others to achieve and realize their full potential. While *Career Killers/Career Builders* is certain to help students and young graduates of all walks of life avoid the most common pitfalls in their careers while offering practical guidance for maximizing success, John's wisdom and life insights will benefit and delight professionals of all ages."

—Craig Robinson, Harvard and
Massachusetts Institute of Technology Graduate

"If you have been looking for a resource that offers an inspirational, insightful, and empowering message about positioning yourself on the path to success and greatness, then you have arrived! John Crossman offers a step-by-step career strategy to building the skills, practices, and values that have helped him as he climbed the corporate ladder. A brilliant communicator and highly sought after speaker, Crossman is a phenomenal storyteller who uses highly entertaining personal life experiences as teachable moments. His generous spirit and his commitment to serving others will move you. Perhaps you have heard the Chinese proverb about giving a man a fish for a day. Well, prepare yourself to learn how to navigate the competitive business environment as John Crossman *teaches you to fish*!"

—Shirley Range, Executive Director, Florida Virtual School Foundation

"John is a true leader in the business world, and he gives sage advice to anyone wanting to walk in his footsteps. His tips are applicable at all levels of business and management. But John's true talent is his ability to inspire and motivate others."

—Bob Braman, Head Coach, Florida State Track
and Cross Country, 2006 and 2008 NCAA Champions

"Thank you for your willingness to impart knowledge that you have ascertained over the years to our next generation of entrepreneurs. The students in the College of Business and Entrepreneurship at Bethune-Cookman University appreciate the time that you have invested in their learning experience over the past five years. We are certain that your book will be just as powerful and impactful as the speech 'Career Killers' was to our faculty, staff, and students of this great institution."

—Ida D. Wright, Dean, College of Business
and Entrepreneurship Bethune-Cookman University

"John Crossman is a successful real estate professional who has also excelled in inspiring students and professionals to take it to the next level. He has put the core of his motivational speech 'Career Killers' into print, which should be a must-read for anyone who wants to succeed."

—Nan Hillis, Retired Banking Executive

"John Crossman is a master at connecting with students in a way that combines common sense, humor, and profound insight. His authenticity is refreshing and rare for a successful CEO, and this is exactly why he captures the attention of his audience. If you are looking for a speaker who will inspire and motivate, John is your guy."

—Jeremy Couch, EdD, Executive Director, Palm Beach Atlantic University

"I would encourage all to read this very great book. This is a must-read for anyone entering the job market. This book is a GPS to success in the workforce with its ever-changing dynamics."

—Belvin Perry Jr., Esq., Morgan & Morgan, PA

"Over the years, I've seen drugs and alcohol ruin many careers, marriages, promising futures, but more importantly, many lives. The road to success will be made incredibly smooth without these two dream killers."

—Sammie Smith, Former NFL Running Back

"I don't know another person in our industry who is more dedicated to making sure students are as prepared as possible to enter the workforce and have a productive, successful career."

—Ron Wheeler, Chief Executive Officer, Sembler

"My first meeting with John followed one of his many speaking engagements with the students of the University of South Florida. During our meeting, John spoke very passionately about his love for students and his outreach to them. So it is only fitting that he continues his outreach via the expansion of his 'Career Killers' speech. In it, students will find the motivation and insight that will empower them to control their own professional destiny."

—Yakhin B. Israel, Vice President,
Commercial Real Estate, Fifth Third Bank

"John Crossman truly cares about the next generation of real estate professionals. He goes above and beyond most people to share his valuable industry wisdom to real estate students. What is unique about his impactful speech, 'Career Killers,' is its applicability to individuals working in any industry at any stage of their careers. This speech motivates students to truly consider their future and take the necessary steps to grow into successful professionals."

—Matthew Rothstein, Commercial Associate

"John Crossman's exceptional ability to motivate students is grounded in his unique and varied experiences as a devout Christian, compassionate spouse and father, esteemed real estate professional, skillful entrepreneur, and former collegiate student-athlete. In his highly acclaimed and insightful work, *Career Killers/Career Builders*, Crossman provides students with valuable inspirational lessons and proven survivals skills to effectively reach their full professional potential."

—Billy R. Close, PhD, Assistant Professor of
Criminology and Criminal Justice, Florida State University

Published by
Union Square Publishing
301 E. 57th Street, 4th floor
New York, NY 10022
www.unionsquarepublishing.com

Manufactured in the United States of America, or in the United Kingdom when distributed elsewhere.

Crossman, John
Career Killers/Career Builders

Paperback: 978-1-938015-69-4
eBook: 978-1-946928-00-9

Cover design by: Joe Potter
Interior design: Scribe, Inc.

http://www.crossmanco.com

This book is dedicated to Dr. Les Kozlow and Dr. Dean Gatzlaff who influenced me in high school and college. I am forever grateful for their support and belief in me.
—*John Crossman*

Table of Contents

Part IV: Creating a Unified Life

Dear Reader

Dear Reader,

From the moment we begin our educational journey, we are asked a very important question: "What do you want to be when you grow up?" I'm sure you remember that teacher who polled the room, asking you and each of your classmates what you envisioned your future to look like. It probably seemed like an innocent question. It offered you the opportunity to be creative and reach for your heart's desires without limitation. You probably heard answers from your classmates like "fireman" and "fairy princess" and "astronaut" and even "basketball player." These were high hopes for each of these dreamers. In kindergarten, you literally get to be anything you want to be. No questions asked. No strings attached. You'll eventually grow those fairy wings.

Time passes and you grow up. If you work hard enough, you graduate high school and enroll in a collegiate education program. You're then likely asked yet again, "What do you want to be when you grow up?" The question is not nearly as casual as it once was because, well, you are getting pretty darn close to actually being a grown-up. In just four years (or five for the victory lappers), you'll be ejected into the real world, hopefully prepared to get a job. If you were lucky enough to receive financial support from your parents, that support will likely come to a screeching halt. Then it is time to truly figure out what's next. Our teachers, loved ones, and friends tell us to get a job. Easier said than done, right? You might feel so confused and unsure of your next steps that you decide to attend *more* school just to put the real world on hold. You might enroll in an MBA program, enter law school, or even start medical school if you are a real glutton for punishment.

But all jokes aside, it is time to exit dreamland and enter reality. If you are on the cusp of the real world, then this book is for you. If you are already in the thick of things, but unsure how to navigate a career, then this book is for you. And if you just need some direction within your chosen career to ensure you continue down the right path, then this book is for you. As we enter the real world, we all need some help. Building a career isn't easy. Keeping it is just as difficult. But it is also not impossible, especially if you are thoughtful with your choices and work to avoid the most substantial landmines that often hide in your path. That is where *Career Killers/Career Builders* comes into play.

This book clarifies what makes people successful. I wrote it to create the biggest impact possible on the next great generation of leaders. I've taken years to study great leaders—the ones who failed, the ones who missed big failure, and the ones who failed and made a comeback. With that in mind, I came up with five career killers and five career builders, all of which will challenge you to think before you make destructive choices. I then turned each of these career killers and career builders into an impactful speech, one that I have given hundreds of times to college students across the country. These students will tell you that the stories that support the lessons are extraordinarily helpful. Since I could only stand in front of so many people at one time, I decided to share these lessons in a more mobile and spreadable manner. That was the foundation for this book.

When asked what I wanted to do when I grew up, I didn't immediately choose "commercial real estate." But for more than twenty years, I have built a successful commercial real estate company. I love what I do. Also, I have used my company as a vehicle to give back to the community by inspiring students to build strong career paths. Not only do I oversee one of the largest retail leasing, management, and development companies in the Southeast, but I teach people just like you, spreading a cutting-edge message about work, life, and success.

I have found passion and purpose in my own career, and I am confident I can help you accomplish the same.

No one enters a career with the intention of getting fired, but it happens every day to well-qualified people in positions where they should logically excel. Sadly, many start their next job only to experience another termination. That doesn't have to be your story. This book will clearly point out what you must avoid and what you must do to ensure that you have a long, successful, and enjoyable career. If you are in college, and especially if you are a junior or senior, your days are numbered. The real world is right around the corner. But that's okay. The real world is pretty awesome. You are close to beginning to recognize financial independence (if you don't already have it) and the ability to grow and develop as a young man or woman. For most of your life, hard work was directly tied to a grade, but now you get to launch your ship to create something even more thrilling. You are about to enter the big leagues.

A great Latin proverb says, "If the wind will not serve, take to the oars." College is like the wind—it takes work, but it moves you through the curriculum and prepares you for your future. But as college comes to an end, you must start paddling your own boat and moving toward your goals. Time to grab those oars, right?

You have come this far, so you are equipped to continue the journey. Likely, you have had plenty of jobs: busboy, pizza delivery person, or cold caller. Those were the fly-by-night opportunities to save a little money and purchase some new shoes or maybe your first car. But we aren't talking jobs here. Together, we are going to build something much more satisfying, more meaningful, and more exciting. As a team, we will help you consider, choose, and succeed in a fulfilling career.

ACKNOWLEDGMENTS

Special thanks: For my family, friends, and staff, thank you for your patience, love and support. In addition, thank you to the numerous college professors who have given me the honor of allowing me to speak to your students. I hope this book will be a resource to all professionals.

PART I

Are You Prepared for the Rest of Your Life?

If you are not prepared for the rest of your life, this book will help you reach that goal. Poet e.e. cummings said, "It takes courage to grow up and become who you really are." As we navigate the top five career killers, you will notice an important theme: The career killers are all avoidable if you act with well-considered thought and an underlying desire to do the right thing the right way. It takes a tremendous amount of time to build your career, and you can end it with just one terrible decision.

Take important steps to prepare your mind and body for the rest of your life. Each day, turn to implementable concepts that can make a tremendous difference in your overall success and growth. Don't settle for ordinary when extraordinary takes just a little more effort and determination.

Are you ready for the rest of your life? If you are just beginning college, or at the end of your educational journey, dig in and begin to consider the answer to this important question. If you feel prepared, this book will help supplement your growth. If you feel like you are lagging even a bit, it will teach you how to move in the right direction.

But no matter where you are in your travels, success starts with knowledge, passion, and maturity, which are the topics of the following chapter.

CHAPTER 1

Building a Career: Knowledge, Passion, Maturity

"There's a time and a place for everything,
and it's called college."

—*Chef from* South Park

College is fun. All types of unbelievable and undeniable fun. I still remember my collegiate days. They were some of the happiest days of my life. You don't need my help to enjoy college— I am confident you can accomplish that on your own. Many have before you, and many will after you. But college can also feel lonely, sad, intimidating, and overwhelming. I will help you navigate the unfamiliar and uncharted world after college. That's where things get, well, a little weird. The real world can seem scary, strange, and will almost certainly prey on plenty of your classmates. But not you. If you have purchased (or borrowed) this book, you are clearly dedicated and determined to move the needle in the direction of success.

Although college students spend thousands on education costs and emerge drowning in student loan debt, many graduates remain unprepared for the workforce. During their collegiate education, they acquire an abundance of knowledge on subjects and receive an inadequate understanding of what will make or break their budding careers. I'm passionate about helping people learn how to make wise choices that will propel them. Whether you're starting your first career job next week or have been employed for five to fifteen years, your decisions will ultimately open doors of opportunity or destroy you. I never want to see anyone fail, especially when it can be avoided with clearheaded thinking and well-thought-out choices.

College is a time to grow, develop, and mature. It is an opportunity to evolve, build strong relationships, and find yourself. You are offered remarkable independence, which some will tell you can be a double-edged sword. But for the occasional check-in call from Mom or Dad, rarely will anyone look over you. And when you speak with your parents, it is quite easy to BS them into thinking all is well, when in reality you are failing chemistry and sold your books to cash in on some extra beer money. But for those of you who have prioritized education and grabbing the bull by the horns, college will give you many of the core fundamental principles to supplement your future growth. At the bare minimum, a college degree will act as a key to unlock the door to your future. Now, more than ever, a collegiate education has become a ticket to enter the ballpark. You get to sit in the stands. Without a college degree, you are standing outside, experiencing the game through the crowd's cheers.

While so many students put their head down and focus on nothing but grades, I want you to do more. As you study, work hard, and set yourself up for success, my goal is to start a new type of conversation. So I have no choice but to ask you that fateful question you've likely been asked before: "What do you want to be *NOW* that you are grown up?"

BUILD A CAREER, NOT A JOB

Some people will tell you that the words "career" and "job" are interchangeable. But from where I sit, they couldn't be more different. If I were to describe the characteristics of a job to you, I would use words like "temporary," "meaningless," "boring," "inconsistent." Now, I am not job bashing. I am just pointing out that jobs are usually what you do because you have to, not because you want to. We obtain jobs to fulfill a personal need, like paying a bill or saving some cash. A career is different. "Purposeful," "passionate," "structured," and "lasting" describe a career. On paper alone, which sounds more valuable to you and your life?

Jobs come and go, but a career is much more lasting and anchored. You go to college to create a career, not to get a job. You might have to a get a job or two along the way to support your collegiate habits, but eventually you move past your job and develop a career. Oftentimes, a career calls upon many of the skills you learned throughout your job history. For example, let's say you become a financial advisor. The skills required include:

- Excellent communication and listening
- The ability to explain complex information clearly and simply
- The ability to analyze and research information
- Good sales-negotiation and report-writing skills
- An interest in financial products and markets

To become a successful financial advisor, you must check each of these crucial boxes. Now, any job may only require just one of these skills, but few would require all of them. Not only is a career much more demanding than a job, it also proves to be much more rewarding. I share this example so you can see just how demanding a successful career may be. But don't get overwhelmed. Your journey through high school and college has set you up for success. Now assemble the puzzle, because I am confident you have all the pieces at your disposal.

CHOOSE WISELY

The rest of this book will focus on the decisions and behaviors that can kill careers and those that can build it. I want you all to be career builders, not career killers. Before we can start the discussion of these killers/builders, I will offer you some guidance on choosing a career. By this point, you likely see the enormous value in picking a career, not just a job. The deeper you get within your career, the more experience and training you'll enjoy. In addition, you'll be more likely to recognize the additional success that goes along with it. That can include a higher salary, greater benefits, and more intrinsic and extrinsic rewards, like a better job title or position and greater responsibility and positive feedback.

So how do you choose a career? I always tell young men and women that a career should accomplish three important goals:

1. It should make you happy.
2. It should highlight your strengths.
3. It should offer you the opportunity to succeed.

If your career does not make you happy, highlight your skillset, and offer you the opportunity to succeed, it might not be a career at all, but it certainly isn't the right career for you. Far too many times, I have spoken with people in their mid-thirties and forties who are completely lost. They aren't personally or professionally happy, and they don't feel successful. As we retrace their steps, inevitably we encounter the notion that their careers are not fulfilling. Even worse, we often realize that they were doomed from the start, mostly because their career choice didn't highlight their strengths or ever excite them. Often, they tell me, "It was the first *job* I was offered." They never even refer to it as a career.

To help you analyze the career you should focus on, answer the following questions. After doing so, review your responses and store them in the back of your mind. As you start career shopping, ask yourself if your strengths are similar to those required to excel in your potential career. So . . . here we go:

My strongest skills and abilities are:

1. _____

2. _____

3. _____

4. _____

5. _____

The areas I would like to improve in the most are:

1. _____

2. _____

3. _____

4. _____

5. _____

From a professional perspective, I am the happiest when I am doing the following:

_____

_____

_____

_____

_____

_____

_____

_____

From a personal perspective, I am the happiest when I am doing the following:

_____

_____

_____

_____

_____

_____

I would define success in my personal life as:

_____

_____

_____

_____

_____

I would define success in my professional life as:

_____

_____

_____

These may seem like simple questions, but we rarely consider them as we dive into the job market. I certainly didn't think about these important points as I jumped into a career. As you leave college, you are so fixated on obtaining a job that you don't even really consider if it is one that could last. I want to help you transform your thinking. Even as a wide-eyed freshman, you should start obtaining clarity surrounding the life you'll have after college. The answers to these questions will help you accomplish just that. So file these answers away, even tear out these pages, and once you start your career search, refresh your memory by glancing at your answers every now and then.

CAREERS TAKE KNOWLEDGE, PASSION, AND MATURITY

Before I start my speech on the top five career killers and builders, I always share with the auditorium of students that you must be three things to secure a meaningful career:

1. Knowledgeable
2. Passionate
3. Mature

Let's unpack each one of them a bit.

Knowledge

Some people refer to this as intelligence, but I prefer the term knowledge because you are born with intelligence but can acquire knowledge. To succeed in any career, you *must* acquire knowledge. You can do this. You're in college, have completed your degree, or are working and want to excel. None of this is accidental—your achievements point to a basic natural intellect.

A key component of knowledge is choosing companions and activities that foster enjoyment of your life's journey and a steadfast pursuit of goals. Those who commit to a group with a common interest transfer that commitment to the course of study they choose. In turn, that camaraderie carries them through tough times and challenges. Knowledgeable people understand this notion.

When I consider the perseverance of the thousands of college students I've worked with, I see how important their participation in a small group was. These were the ones who typically stayed connected throughout their time at the university. Their small community supported a "do not quit" mindset. Many kinds of groups foster this spirit of perseverance: a sorority or fraternity, a band, a sport, a church organization, or even friends who get together regularly based on a common interest. The company of likeminded friends indicates your natural intelligence and reinforces your intention to learn and succeed.

You can then supplement these experiences with studying hard and working to become an expert in a specific subject matter. For example, most colleges require that you designate a major or a specific area you plan to focus on during your time in college. This is a great tool because it pushes you to announce a preferred area of study to the world. After making that decision, you get to hone your craft and focus on the core curriculum that will help you acquire a great deal of knowledge.

For instance, you may want to go into public relations after college. To get prepared, you enroll in a communications school and focus on marketing, writing, media, and other pertinent subjects. While you may not get the real-world experience of working as a PR specialist, you will acquire an intimate understanding of what it takes to get the job done. You will leave college knowledgeable and ready to jump right into the world of work.

Robert Gidel of Liberty Capital Advisors shared this with me: "The only way to build your human capital is to gain knowledge and experience, both of which come from the personal interaction with those from whom we can learn. There is no substitute for creating and using personal connections in this process. It won't come from faceless Internet, social media, or email communications. Only through consistent and persistent pursuit of knowledge gained through personal conversations with experienced professionals can one separate himself and add value in this extremely competitive world."

Passion

Passion is extraordinarily important. We all do better when we are passionate about what we are doing. How many times did you get excited about doing your homework? How about taking out the trash? Pretty boring and mundane stuff, right? But what about that time you participated in the marketing fair? Remember when you got the opportunity to create and market a new and unique product? I bet you went all in. You couldn't stop thinking about it. You constantly brainstormed with friends. You wouldn't shut up about your pitch. That's passion in play. And it really works. I want the same for you and your career.

Passion is simply a desire to do great things. Not everyone is passionate about everything. That's not true of every college student or employee, because some are just floating around. But it is true of you. A look around will reveal things that block success for people. Apathy and discouragement stand out as great enemies of achievement. So often, if people simply make an effort, pursue passion, and apply themselves, they'll succeed.

A lack of intelligence doesn't hold them back—not caring does. Intelligence, passion, and maturity are the basic traits you need. Even if you haven't employed these traits for maximum effectiveness, you can make better choices. Although most people see me as a positive guy, I've had moments of apathy and discouragement.

In those moments, three things helped me.

1. First, I made a disciplined choice to keep everything in perspective.
2. Second, I learned to embrace failure as part of the process.
3. Third, I received tremendous support from friends who kept me focused, supported me, and were my cheering section when my score was low.

At every level of success, I think about the movie *Castaway* with Tom Hanks. The character he played was stranded on an island with no reason to think he'd make it out alive. The day after his lowest level, when he considers killing himself, a big piece of plastic washes up on shore. Later in the movie, he says, "You never know what the tide brings in."

There's truth in that. When we work hard, discipline ourselves, and strive to make the right decisions, sometimes things come our way. Remember that feelings are temporary. In the same way that great moments of joy fade, so will the times of deep sadness. Remind yourself that tomorrow *is* a fresh start and stay focused on the core things. Keep doing them.

Most runners come to a hill and slow down because they know it's always easier to run down the other side. Instead, I try to attack the hills and run faster. When I ran competitively, I could always catch up and beat people when I pushed myself and ran up the hills harder than everyone else. The same is true for life. Passion for what you are doing allows you to tackle that hill like no other.

So it is extremely important that you choose a career that excites you and that you desire. Inevitably, you will feel passion, and you will, therefore, fulfill your daily responsibilities in a highly effective way. When the going gets tough, passion will be even more crucial to your overall ability to overcome obstacles.

Maturity

Maturity is a big one. Many of the career killers often stem from immature decision making. Coming out of college, we expect you to continue your development and mature. I did. I am much more mature now than I was in college. I am much more mature now than I was before getting married. I am much more mature now than I was before owning a business. And I am much more mature now than I was before having kids or even a dog. Those are some significant wake-up calls. Because as your responsibility grows, so should your maturity.

My wife and I have two daughters. When the older one turned nine and had her first slumber party, it was awesome. No, I didn't get any sleep, but they had fun. At that time, my youngest was seven. Because daughters are only one grade apart in school, they share many friends, and the whole family had a blast. That party reminded me of when we were new parents. Our church had a class, which opened with this question: "What is the goal of parenting?"

That's a great question, I thought. *I have no idea. It's probably something I should have thought about before I started having kids.* The instructor said the goal was to teach maturity. I nodded and thought that was cool. Then he said, "What is maturity?" When I was growing up and heard people say, "That person is immature," it offended me. I thought when people called others immature, *they* were immature. I didn't understand what they meant. Maturity is the combination of three things:

1. Self-control
2. Wisdom
3. Responsibility

Each of these is crucial to developing into a mature individual, professionally and personally. Let's look at each one.

SELF-CONTROL

When you're raising kids, one of the first things you teach them is to control their impulses. If your family is sitting at the dinner table and there are cookies on a plate in easy reach, your kids will grab some unless you've taught them that they must eat their dinner first, including vegetables. Afterward they can have a cookie. This is a simple way to teach them self-control.

In a situation with anger, you can explain, "When you get mad at your sister, don't punch her in the face. Instead, come and tell Mom and Dad." Why do you tell them this? Because kids are all emotion all the time. Instinctively, they react to what goes on around them, so you should teach them how to respond through your words and actions. They don't come by it automatically. Those who grow up without the benefit of this kind of consistent, caring instruction often have great gaps in their self-control, and this creates dangerous chasms of poor behavior.

WISDOM

You gain wisdom by learning from your mistakes. When you do something and have a painful outcome, you usually don't do it again. For example, you tell your kid not to touch a hot stove to avoid getting burned. After the first time the kid touches it, he doesn't do it a second time.

On a recent vacation, a yellow jacket stung my younger daughter. From now on, she's going to be very careful around wasps and bees. That one incident instilled specific wisdom: the lifelong knowledge to be careful around insects. This knowledge and vivid experience will extend to other things; she'll learn to apply caution elsewhere.

RESPONSIBILITY

Responsibility means acknowledging your actions. When my second daughter was very young, she had chocolate all over her mouth, and I asked, "Ava, did you eat a chocolate chip cookie?" "No," she answered, but she looked away. That's what kids do. They lie. By teaching them to admit to their actions, they learn personal responsibility.

Sometimes when you call out your kids, they lie, and you have to say, "You lied about that. You have to say you're sorry. You have to accept responsibility. No, you don't get dessert tonight and no, you can't stay up later, because you made a mistake and you're going to get punished for that. But tomorrow's a new day, and you can start all over."

Apply this definition of maturity to evaluate behavior in society. When I work with prison inmates, I see a variety of issues related to immaturity. Many incarcerated people would get poor marks for their self-control, choices, and willingness to be held accountable and make appropriate changes in behavior.

For instance, prisoners often strike out at others from long-practiced habits. "Well, I didn't like that guy, so I punched him in the face." These unchecked attitudes and actions often lead to felony convictions and prison. Many repeat offenders never learned to avoid the negative consequences of reacting and overreacting, so they keep doing the same things.

Often, I find that theses inmates had no father in their home. One common consequence of parental absence is a failure to learn these components of maturity: self-control, wise choices, and responsibility. That's why it's important to instill behaviors that lead to success. If these disruptive traits aren't changed, they become deeply ingrained, continue into adulthood, and show up in the workplace.

People who get fired often share a common trait: It's not that they aren't smart, or don't care, but typically they lack maturity. They just aren't willing to make responsible decisions. Being smart with facts or skills won't sustain a long-term career when these three components of maturity are missing. Unchecked, the individual will make the same mistakes in work habits and work relationships. Although they're good employees in many ways, they bounce from job to job. Why? Because they don't see that *they* are the common factor in having to start over.

Personal responsibility is a powerful trait. Many people refuse to say, "I made a mistake" because it's too hard for them to admit a flaw. They view any admission of error as weakness, believing that their position is one of strength and power. Think about people you've met or known with that outlook. They tell themselves they've never made a mistake in their lives, never admit they're wrong, or take responsibility for their choices. That's a real problem.

A few years ago, my brother and I had a big issue in our accounting department. Having problems in accounting while running your business is like trying to change the oil in your car when you're driving down the interstate. It's very hard to adjust accounting while the company is moving forward with its day-to-day business. This problem was stressing us out. In the middle of discussing it with my brother, he looked at me and said, "You know whose fault this is?" I was surprised and asked, "Whose?" "Mine," he answered.

I wasn't expecting that, but when he took responsibility, it empowered me and made me feel good. I really appreciated his admission. Later, we were having problems in our leasing and marketing department, which is my division. I said to him, "You know whose fault this is? This is mine." An important quality of a mature person is the willingness to say, "Hey, my mistake. Not some other guy's. Not another person's. This is my problem. I accept personal responsibility." When we hire students, a key quality we seek in them is maturity, because it's critical for healthy employees. Immaturity is like sand in suntan lotion, a constant irritant that affects the mood and tone of the work environment. Poor impulse control, failure to accept responsibility, and unwillingness to be accountable contribute to getting fired beyond the other reasons, such as not fulfilling your job responsibilities and company downsizing.

So there you have it: self-control, wisdom, and responsibility—the three most important traits to start a career. When you possess these traits, you can navigate the forthcoming changes in your life. Without them, you will have trouble finding and inevitably keeping a career. Likely, you will get lost on the path of job after job after job. They might pay the bills, but there's no chance they'll fulfill your basic human desires and goals. And once you find that career, the rest of this book is going to help you keep it.

PART II

The Career Killers

We all strive to create a meaningful life, filled with tremendous opportunity and success. As we survey our potential, we start to consider the steps we can all take to manifest a wonderful personal and professional life. But rarely do we consider those decisions that can completely derail it all. Just one lapse in judgment can result in catastrophic results. We refer to these moments as *Career Killers*.

This section of the book will help you to not only identify *Career Killers*, but also move them to the top of your mind, so you can work to constantly avoid them. Actor Will Rogers said, "Good judgment comes from experience, and a lot of that comes from bad judgment." Now that might just be the case, but we live in a world where even one instance of bad judgment can cost you everything for which you've worked. So together, let's take an important journey through some of the most dangerous behaviors and decisions you can make (or even not make).

In the end, you have one life to live. Make it count. *Here's how . . .*

CHAPTER 2

Career Killer #1

DRUGS AND ALCOHOL: NO ONE LIKES THE LIFE OF THE PARTY AFTER THE PARTY

"Oh no! What have I done? I smashed open my little
boy's piggy bank and for what? A few measly cents,
not even enough to buy one beer. Wait a minute,
lemme count and make sure . . . not even close."

—*Homer Simpson*

This probably isn't a remarkable surprise to you, but here goes: The number one career killer is drugs and alcohol. Plain and simple. We'd love for them to make our lives be like a movie, with an epic party scene followed by the most wonderful night ever, but most times mind-altering substances lead to disaster. In college, being the life of the party could almost certainly be directly linked to how much alcohol you consumed, how much drugs you could handle in one sitting and, of course, all the terrible decisions you made to entertain yourself and your friends. There was a time when you could be socially accepted for being the drunkest gal or guy at the bar.

But that time is gone, and drugs and alcohol can kill your career. If you regularly read the news, or enjoy social media outlets, a day doesn't go by without yet another public figure damaging his or her reputation, or even worse, dying, because of their dependency on drugs and alcohol. Sometimes it doesn't even take a real substance abuse problem. One bad night can lead to a lifetime of ramifications. Just ask the professional athlete who drove drunk and killed another person, the entertainer who got his mistress pregnant, the CEO who texted "one of those pictures" to a girlfriend who posted it on the Web, and sadly, the young man or woman who overdosed from a single taking of drugs. Heck, I can't even tell you how many times I've seen a professional get way too drunk at a holiday party and say something he or she regrets the next day. The stories are not just tragic, they seem to be endless too. Likely, we can all remember that one colleague who took it too far and recognized some serious consequences because of it.

Back to college. College people tend to do crazy things. I get that. But when I think about college, I always remember the following quote: "When I was a child, I spoke like a child, I thought like a child, I reasoned like a child. When I became a man, I gave up childish ways." The first part of the quote points to irresponsible choices, while the second part describes the progression from childish behaviors to maturity. College is a great place to mature and develop, but I hope that you have sown your wild oats and compartmentalized the fun. As you exit college and enter a profession, you must reduce and minimize your alcohol use and eliminate the use of any drugs without valid treatment reasons and recommendation from a doctor.

College is wonderful because it offers a time of transition. You can spread your wings, expand your horizons, and assert your independence. It also allows you to try things, and for many college students, that means alcohol and drugs. Think about this and address common college mistakes so you don't take them forward with you. Picture yourself ten years from now. You've graduated from the university, gotten a job, but then gotten fired because of inappropriate drinking or use of drugs.

Would you regret the decisions you made leading up to this?
Would you curse that "one bad night"?
Would you blame alcohol and/or drugs?

Here's the truth: You would have no one to blame but yourself. You'll be much better off subscribing to the notion that an ounce of prevention is much better than a pound of cure. That said, let's talk in more detail about how drugs and alcohol will completely derail your career and even your life.

YOU CAN RUN, BUT YOU CAN'T HIDE

I can still remember Jane, a young woman who worked for us. She had always been considered a rising star in the industry. As a nondrinker, I don't tend to notice excessive drinking, but people who like to party hard do. Jane drank too much at a company event, so much so that she went to the women's restroom and threw up everywhere. Obviously, I wasn't there, but the story was repeated for years. It became part of her reputation, and everyone knew Jane as the girl who got so sick she threw up at the company party. For a host of reasons, I am sure she regretted drinking that much. Funny enough, the colleagues most disgusted by her actions were those who partied hard but knew how to set limits on themselves.

Jane likely didn't think of the potential outcomes for her behavior. She probably had one drink, then another, then lost all inhibitions and couldn't shut it down. If only she had stopped after one or two. Take the time to understand the potential outcome of this behavior. A long time ago, I worked with a guy who had a reputation for having "the shakes." I didn't know what that meant, but thought it was odd he always had a super Big Gulp on his desk and was constantly sipping it. He was actually drinking alcohol throughout the day. Everyone in the office talked about his alcoholism, but he was unaware that they knew. Over time, his unaddressed problem not only limited his opportunities but also led to a divorce. Do you want a substance abuse issue as your calling card? Probably not. I know plenty of thirty-year-olds with hilarious tales to tell of college drunkenness. But if those same drunken stories took place at a work function, they wouldn't be funny at all. They would be sad. These behaviors indicate a lack of self-control and signal immaturity and poor judgment. They may even indicate a substance abuse problem, which can derail an otherwise successful career.

In the early 2000s, the *Orlando Business Journal* ran a list of quotes of the year. When I found out they picked one of mine, it was kind of cool. They quoted me saying, "Christmas parties are work, not parties. Don't get fired after having too much eggnog." The truth in those words is clear the first time you hear them. If someone says there's a party, you might think party equals drunkenness. It's likely you know someone who thinks that way. However, when you hear the word party, this is the actual equation: *Work party plus drunkenness equals fired.* So be sure to keep the right outlook. If you're going to a function that's a work event with an open bar, that's cool. Have one beer or glass of wine—the formula for self-control. Always remember, you're not there to party, you're there to work. If there's an open bar, it's offered for your convenience and in appreciation of your attendance. It's not an invitation to get trashed.

Because I don't drink, I don't know how to gauge when someone's had too much. I don't feel judgmental about drinking—I just don't have a sensitivity to it. However, I've noticed that some of my friends who are my age, in their forties, still party hard, which is sad. It's time to get past that. However, those people are the very ones who are judgmental of others who get drunk at company functions.

My friends have the discernment and the self-control to restrict the places where they indulge in alcohol. They reason, "If it's Saturday night and I'm with my friends, I can do whatever I want. On the other hand, if I'm at work or at a company function, I don't do that." Step back and evaluate your own patterns. Be brutally honest. You matter. Your career and family matter. You may need to make some changes.

TOEING THE LINE

Look, I am not a prude. I am not saying you should never drink. There is a time and a place for everything. For example, there is no harm in a couple of beers after work, or a glass of wine with dinner, or a cocktail at a party. They usually go hand in hand with networking and people connecting. Many folks drink socially. There's nothing wrong with that. But when social drinking increases, it ceases to be "social" and can become a problem. You don't have to be an alcoholic or a drug addict for substance abuse to negatively or even devastatingly impact your career. Just think of Jane and her "one too many."

Now drugs are an entirely different conversation. I get that people do drugs. If you do, stop. Stop it now. And if you can't, get help immediately. I cannot tell you how many people I have seen who completely wrecked their careers with a cocaine or OxyContin addiction. I've seen very successful people do this. I've seen people my age make a ton of money, then completely lose their careers and become homeless. Drugs are extraordinarily difficult, because they are extremely addictive, even more so than alcohol. It is unlikely you'll be addicted to alcohol after just one drink. But there are drugs that can completely wipe you out after just one dose.

A guy I used to work with was regarded as one of the top three most influential people in his respective industry. He was described as young (he was in his mid-thirties), hot, and one of the brightest up-and-comers. But he made me uneasy. He was good looking and hard working. Often, he was the first one in the office, but he tended to leave every day around four o'clock, which I found odd. But I thought maybe he enjoyed going to the gym or hanging with friends.

Strangely enough, his confidence had an off-putting level of arrogance. For example, in meetings, he always sat at the head of the table opposite the managing partner as if he were equal to him. But it was more than that. I was just twenty-two, but when I read an article about the personality habits of people with drug addiction, those traits reminded me of him. So I read the article to numerous people in the office, without identifying it as cocaine addiction behavior. I then asked them if the traits described in the article sounded like they belonged to anyone they knew. Every person said they reminded him or her of this same guy.

Eventually, he had to take time off work to have nasal surgery. Then, it became more obvious there was a serious problem. Strangely, our boss didn't seem to care. I assumed this employee was making a lot of money for the company, so they ignored the telltale signs. One day, his very attractive wife, who was pregnant, came by the office with their two kids. While she was there, the most disturbing thing I'd ever witnessed at work occurred. While holding their youngest, who was less than a year old, the man started taunting and smacking his baby. He hit the baby in the arm, and while his slap didn't leave a bruise, the baby started crying. I didn't believe my eyes.

Again, nothing happened. Later on, he got busted for having sex with a prostitute and doing drugs with another man in a building he managed. Even after that, he wasn't fired. The last time I talked to him, he admitted that he was a cocaine addict and had gotten help for it. I haven't heard much from him in the last ten years. This is a sad story of how drug addiction can literally ruin your life. He could have had it all. In fact, he really did. But he traded it for his love of drugs. He'd had a lovely wife and two beautiful children, but lost them in a divorce. While that wasn't the end of the world, he then lost his career.

Before his life fell apart, you could have asked him, "What do you value most?" He probably would have said, "My family, my wife, my children, and my career." In reality, he chose a white powder over each one of them and lost everything. Maybe his story eventually became one of redemption and recovery. But my goal is to keep you from going down that dark road in the first place.

CAREER RECOVERY

Not everyone succumbs to substance abuse or the ramifications of it. There are plenty of success stories about people who have had problems with alcohol or drugs and recovered mightily. If you feel you have a problem with alcohol or drugs, the first step is to work toward finding the support you need to bounce back and overcome these issues.

My uncle came from a bad background. He and my mom had rough childhoods. I was unaware of this until she spoke at his funeral. She said, "Many of you think we were raised by wolves, but you're wrong, because that would imply that we had parents."

I came to find out that they really grew up on the street. My uncle said that the first time he felt normal was the first time he got drunk. When he married Aunt Sandy, a beautiful and wonderful woman, she did what she could to help him. Finally, she drew a line in the sand and divorced him.

When my uncle tried to figure out what to do about his alcoholism, he went to talk to his neighbor John. This was unusual because he didn't like John and referred to him as a jerk. But John went to Alcoholics Anonymous and agreed to sponsor my uncle, and this act of kindness led to almost forty years of sobriety. During that time, my uncle sponsored dozens of people and helped them get through a variety of tough issues. This is just one example of someone recovering from deep alcoholism. He not only saved his career, he saved his life. Additionally, he and his wife reconciled and were married for fifty-three years.

The truth is that people never think drugs or alcohol will ruin their lives when they start using. I've seen people become extraordinarily wealthy, only to get addicted to cocaine and then find themselves homeless. White-collar, professional businesspeople have ruined their lives with alcohol and drugs. I guarantee you that they all thought, *That will never happen to me.*

A close friend of mine is a minister. I'm so proud of the life he leads and the work he does, but I'm more proud that he overcame a devastating addiction and got his life back on track. Here is his story in his own words:

I started drinking and partying when I was thirteen. By nineteen or twenty, I was using a lot of cocaine and other drugs.

From twenty-four to thirty, my major drug problem was cocaine—a six-year addiction. Much of my early professional career was spent in the technology business working for an international tech company as an area sales manager. I started out intensely focused, trying to work my way up the corporate ladder. However, as my addiction got worse, my job performance and production became very inconsistent. The district manager observed my behavior and talked to me about cleaning myself up.

I continued to use, and over time I missed more and more days of work. To help me, my manager let me shift to a major account sales role where I wouldn't be responsible for an entire sales team, but only my own sales. Once again, I started out with excellent production, but foolishly funneled the high income into my escalating cocaine and alcohol addiction. After a four-day alcohol and cocaine binge when I never called in to work, I was terminated.

I got another job and concealed my drug habit for a while. However, the drugs kept me in an agitated state, and I frequently argued with my boss. That job ended. My third opportunity was in the mortgage business at the height of the market. I was running a company and didn't report to anyone. In fact, I only checked in with the owners once a month. The job itself enabled me to get worse. I considered my $20,000 monthly paycheck as a gauge of how much I could party. Needless to say, I got fired again.

The cycle of addiction that leads to job loss after job loss escalates the pressure with each new position to do well, because each time could be the last shot at a good job. Like other addicts, I tricked myself into feeling I could handle it, only to go back to using. Then I was brought into a tech company in an introductory role. They were willing to overlook my past. For a short time, I felt that I better not mess up. I knew I had blown it, but I didn't want to admit it, so I worked hard to cut back on partying. But once I got comfortable, my drug and alcohol use escalated again. It was only a matter of time before I was confronted.

Drugs made me feel invincible, even delusional. I convinced myself that play hard/work hard go hand in hand, as long as I met my sales goals. I didn't consider it substance abuse— I thought of it as a lifestyle. My addiction affected my coworkers. Most of them knew about it; many got drunk with me, but few were willing to do cocaine. My boss knew what was going on because the sales reps knew I was partying. I was in management, and the people who reported to me had to deal with someone whose emotions were all over the place. One day I'd be great—the next day, I'd be out of my mind and trying to have serious business conversations. Sadly, I was arrogant enough to think it was okay.

My friend was lucky. He got clean and sober and got his life back on track. But looking back over my career, I knew other gifted, successful career people who died of drug overdoses. I've seen it time and time again. Don't let it happen. As I said earlier, stop. Stop now.

HEALTH KILLER

Alcohol and drugs are not just a career killer but also a health killer. They can lead to serious health conditions, if not death. And in each of those continued battles, there is generally a great deal of money lost and dollars spent. The National Council on Alcoholism and Drug Dependence Inc. reported that drug abuse costs employers $81 billion annually. Aside from the legal ramifications of drug possession and the potential for health complications resulting from their abuse, drugs are an expensive habit. The more addicted someone gets, the more expensive their drug habit gets. The more it costs, the more temptation a person faces to make devastating choices to support the habit.

Drug abuse can cause problems at work including:

- Aftereffects of substance use (withdrawal) affecting job performance
- Preoccupation with obtaining and using substances while at work, interfering with attention, and concentration
- Illegal activities at work including selling illegal drugs to other employees
- Psychological or stress-related effects due to drug use by a family member, friend, or coworker that affects another person's job performance[1]

They can also come with the potential to money spent via legal troubles. I have heard many stories of the "one too many" leading to a driving under the influence charge (DUI) or other serious arrest. If you are regularly purchasing drugs, you could easily be arrested for simple possession or something even worse. The possession of any other drug besides marijuana is generally a felony in most states. Those include prescription medications for which you do not possess a valid prescription. Even if you haven't known someone whose use and eventual abuse of illegal or prescription drugs led to criminal activity, many stories support this.

A felony conviction can make it difficult to get another job, take away your right to vote, deny you access to gun ownership, and even keep you from traveling to other countries. Some countries deny felons access to cross their borders, but others, including Canada, count *all* criminal convictions—even DUIs—as a basis to deny entry.

Curtailing your rights isn't the only cost of substance abuse. Legal fees related to drug arrests can bankrupt you. Even a first DUI can be costly. In Florida, the Department of Motor Vehicles estimates the average cost of a first offense DUI, including attorney fees, fines, and increases in auto insurance premiums, is $8,000. The national average is $10,000.

---

1   National Council on Alcoholism and Drug Dependence Inc.

The Florida Institute of Technology reports that alcohol and drug use contributes to 60 percent of all substandard job performance and at least 40 percent of all industrial accidents.

A friend suffered some health problems and took doctor-prescribed prescription drugs. This led to abuse and inappropriate business dealings. When he began to overcharge in his business, it became clear he was supporting a drug habit, which led to him losing his job. People fool themselves. They think they can hide or control their addiction, but eventually it catches up to them. That's why, for instance, at the first hint you "need" additional drugs if you've been on pain medication, you should get help.

Just because a drug is legal doesn't mean it's safe. Each person responds differently to drugs. However, it's wise to follow your doctor's instructions exactly, even if you decide to get a second opinion. The second doctor may adjust your medication or treatment, but avoid the temptation to change the dosage or frequency in contradiction to the instructions of a professional.

I learned that taking any prescribed medications *can* present issues. I have a high tolerance for pain. On a vacation with my wife, my back went into severe spasms and I had to be hospitalized because I couldn't move. Because of my pain and resulting impaired mental state, I wasn't paying attention to the multiple pain meds they put me on. When I sobered up, I realized I was simultaneously taking Valium, OxyContin, and steroids.

I called a friend who was a doctor and read him the list of meds I was taking. He was stunned. I quit them cold turkey, which caused a lot of stress. I probably should have gradually reduced them and then stopped, but I didn't want to become dependent on them in any capacity.

For more than ten years, opiate abuse has been an epidemic in our country. In many cases, doctors at "pill mills" readily write prescriptions for addictive pain pills and ancillary drugs, such as Xanax, to build an addicted client base for ongoing business. Prescription drug addiction can be very expensive. I've seen it turn honest people into thieves, desperate to support their habit by any means necessary. They often start with pain pills and then find themselves needing a stronger fix. It can then end with an injectable like heroin.

I'm not saying that doctors who prescribe pain medication are unethical, nor am I saying pain medication isn't necessary. But wisdom dictates we exercise rigorous restraint with any prescription drug. Thoroughly discuss side effects with your physician and determine a timeline for taking it—and adhere to it. Appropriate treatment for pain should include identifying and treating the source of the pain through physical therapy or other means. If your doctor doesn't recommend treatment for the source, find another doctor.

DEATH OF YOUR CAREER

It goes without saying that being drunk or stoned in the workplace is simply not acceptable. It can negatively affect the quality of your work, your interactions with customers and coworkers, the safety of your workplace, and your reputation. In the workplace, the impact of alcoholism focuses on four major issues:

- Premature death/fatal accidents
- Injuries/accident rates
- Absenteeism/extra sick leave
- Loss of production[2]

Even worse, employees who abuse drugs and alcohol cost employers through:

- Tardiness/sleeping on the job
- Theft
- Poor decision making
- Loss of efficiency

---

2   National Council on Alcoholism and Drug Dependence Inc.

- Lower morale of coworkers
- Increased likelihood of having trouble with coworkers/ supervisors or tasks
- Higher turnover
- Training of new employees
- Disciplinary procedures[3]

I am sure you'd agree any one of these issues is substantial enough to result in termination. But when it comes to alcohol or drugs, there is usually a mix of many of these issues. What you decide to do on the weekends is your business, but how it affects you on Monday morning is your employer's business. Showing up to work hung over or fuzzyheaded from a binge weekend will make it impossible to deliver your peak performance. You'll do yourself a disservice and put a burden on your coworkers to pick up your slack while you nurse your pounding headache.

PROTECTING YOUR REPUTATION

At the end of the day, this really boils down to protecting your reputation. Sure, alcohol and drugs are career killers, but they are also reputation killers. Try working in the same industry after losing your current job because of drugs or alcohol. People talk, and you shouldn't be surprised just how quickly one bad night can spread. Even if your alcohol intake doesn't result in a calamitous event, it can have a negative effect on your reputation. It's much easier to build and keep a good reputation than it is to overcome a bad one. Work parties and work-related events often include spouses. It's just as important that your husband, wife, or significant other use the same degree of discretion. Their behavior reflects directly on you and on your reputation.

Now, you probably understand why the first career killer discussed in this book relates directly to alcohol and drug abuse.

---

3   National Council on Alcoholism and Drug Dependence Inc.

It might be the least common issue most readers face, but it is easily the most detrimental. If you do not regularly use alcohol or drugs, then your focus should simply be on maintaining composure and limiting your alcohol intake during professional and work-related endeavors. This isn't college. The goal is not necessarily to be the life of the party.

If you think you may have a problem, the Florida Institute of Technology publishes a quick test to gauge whether your substance abuse is considered an addiction. Consider the following:

- Have you ever felt like you should decrease your drinking and/or drug use?
- Have you ever felt annoyed by criticism of your drinking and/or drug use?
- Have you ever felt guilty about drinking, using drugs, or how you behave when you're drunk/stoned?
- Do you ever have a drink or use drugs in the morning?

The Institute indicates that if you answered yes to only two of these questions, you are likely dependent on drugs or alcohol. If you answered yes to three or four of the questions, there is more than a 95 percent chance that you are addicted. Now, we all know a small questionnaire is unlikely to accurately evaluate you without more information, but I would suggest you consider affirmative answers to these questions as potential warning signs. It is much better to be aware and hypersensitive to these issues than to realize you have a problem once it is too late.

If you do determine you have a problem, begin facing it head on and know there is a great deal of love and compassion around you for support. Overcoming addiction is hard, but it's worth it. If you feel you have a problem with drugs or alcohol, or may be on your way to having a problem, get help *now*. The chances of overcoming it on your own are slim at best. Do it for yourself, for your family, and for your career. Some steps I recommend you take include:

- Calling your local chapter of Alcoholics Anonymous, Narcotics Anonymous, or Cocaine Anonymous to find out their meeting schedule closest and most convenient for you.
- Ask your family doctor for a referral to a treatment center or counselor that can help.
- Discuss your situation with your clergyperson or religious leader, and ask if there are options available through your church or other religious affiliation for substance abuse problems.

These are just a few resources you have at your disposal. But it is your responsibility alone to determine if you have an issue, and most importantly, to address it. Remember, most of you likely do not have issues with substance abuse, but this doesn't mean "one too many" won't change the course of your career. You graduated high school, studied hard in college, and did all you could to begin a career early in your life. Don't blow it because of one bad night and a few too many. While alcohol and drugs can have the greatest impact on the course of your career, you also retain the greatest control over this issue. There is no mystery here. Overindulge and risk your career. Make responsible decisions, and you will maintain focus and a strong trajectory.

CHAPTER 3

Career Killer #2

SEX: MONOGAMY IS MAGNIFICENT

"I don't know the question, but sex is definitely the answer."

—*Woody Allen*

The workplace is great for socializing, building friendships, creating relationships, and getting to know your colleagues. But it is, without a shadow of a doubt, not the place to look for love. Just say no to workplace romance. There are plenty of ponds in which to fish, so don't bother fishing in your professional career. To be blunt, don't have sex with people you work with. Even worse, if you do make the mistake of getting involved with a work colleague, don't compound the issue by getting intimate with someone who is married or has a significant other. That behavior is a recipe for disaster, and there is no good result. It is not like a fairytale where you fall in love and ride into the sunset together. It is more like a complete and utter disaster just waiting to happen. The fire is burning, and you are about to toss a gallon of gasoline on it.

I'm a big fan of the TV show *The Office*. The characters are constantly dating in the workplace. They just cannot get enough of one another. I can completely understand it, and it makes for great television. Every now and again, the relationships end well. However, I'd simply advise you to be very cautious as you navigate these choppy waters. First, I consider office dating lazy dating. The thought is, "Well, she's there." That is not a good reason to date anybody. Second, you're there to work. I've seen outstanding young people severely limit their careers because they started dating someone in the workplace, which led to work-related issues and problems. You can become distracted, disengaged, emotional, jealous, and even caught red-handed by your boss. Most businesses even have a policy against dating your colleagues, so be aware that even one date could lead to the loss of your job.

That really is just more of a conversation in self-control. Just because you find a coworker attractive doesn't mean you need to date that individual. There are a lot of great people you'll find interesting and be attracted to, but you don't have to date and sleep with them. I am not saying don't date, socialize, and enjoy yourself. I am not even saying don't have sex. You can date people from other places. In fact, you really should. Building a loving relationship is one of the most rewarding experiences for us as human beings. But put some effort into meeting new people and think through the choice of workplace dating and its possible (negative) outcomes. Here are just some of the issues that come with dating your married (or even single) coworkers, or even just allowing sex to become a theme or topic of conversation in the office:

Relationships with Married Coworkers. One of my friends, a good guy in many ways, had a salary of about a half a million dollars a year and enjoyed awesome perks like a company jet. But he was having an affair with the director of marketing, who was married. Although people found out, it didn't really become an issue until his wife contacted his CEO. In turn, my friend and his paramour were fired. His story offers a warning, as his career never recovered. If he'd made some adjustments and dealt with the issues in his marriage, maybe his situation would have worked out differently. But that wasn't the only fallout from this ill-advised relationship. In addition to the issue of cheating on her husband, the director of marketing was not meeting expectations in her own job. She thought her liaison with a C-suite executive made her bulletproof, so she quit fulfilling her daily responsibilities. Everyone around her became less effective, and it became a very dysfunctional workplace. Unfortunately, I've seen this pattern again and again.

Embarrassment in the Office. It is easy to send the wrong message to your coworkers when you are dating one of them. A couple of women I worked with resigned after being at their company for a long time. Their departure was awkward, especially because they went to work for a client and took some business with them. However, because of the length of their employment, the boss decided to give them a going-away party.

The party took place in a conference room without a table, so they sat in the center of a large open space, receiving gifts from their colleagues. There was a door behind them.

To come in or out of the room, you had to walk in front of them, making any entrance or exit somewhat awkward. As the celebration was underway, all the employees formed a semi-circle around them while they opened presents provided by the company.

Keep in mind, they were expecting gold watches or something extravagant. The boss, who wasn't going to be there, chose to delegate the party plans and gift buying to an employee. That wasn't the best exercise of judgment. He thought that by sending along a second employee with good judgment, it would balance the possible poor choices of the initial party planner. It didn't.

When the first employee went in a questionable direction, the second wasn't strong enough to stop it. So picture a downtown office in the middle of the day, with a room full of employees gathered around two women expecting gold watches. Penis-shaped pasta was the first gift the women opened. A penis-shaped thermos was the second gift. I don't recall the third, but you can likely guess the theme of it.

While attending that party, I stood next to a nineteen-year old intern. I was horrified, along with everyone in the room, and especially the two female gift recipients. Immediately, I walked to my desk and ordered a bouquet of flowers for each woman with my own money. A note accompanied the flowers congratulating them on their new jobs. Then I called my boss and said, "I don't know how you're *not* going to have a lawsuit on your hands."

Almost twenty years later, I walked into a meeting. The receptionist turned out to be the woman who had bought all the penis-related objects. As I left the meeting, she pulled me aside and asked for a word. She told me she'd been a cocaine addict back then and admitted she'd done rather mean things to me and to others. She had joined Narcotics Anonymous and wanted to make amends and apologize. I couldn't remember her doing anything to me, but that conversation explained a lot. It also serves as a great example of two career killers: drugs and sex.

Most times, drugs and alcohol don't lead directly to work-related lawsuits. But sex is a different story. I've seen bright people lose their reputation and expose their companies to substantial sexual harassment lawsuits. If you're an employee faced with an opportunity to make an unwise choice, just say "no," because the fallout can be substantial. If you're an employer, don't cross the line. It's never the secret you think it is. Everybody knows. Every last one of them. I can't tell you the number of times I've seen people go to great lengths to keep their affairs a secret while everyone around them knew exactly what was going on. If you need to keep a relationship secret, you should probably seriously question why you're in it in the first place.

It Doesn't Just Affect You and Your Partner. Work-related affairs don't just impact you and your family. The decisions you make at work affect everything and everyone around you. How you process them can then have a remarkable impact on your life. For years, I worked in a very stressful office. The managing director ran the place like a middle-school-boys' locker room, where his private inner group teased and made fun of others, ruling the office like bullies. No one received encouragement for doing a good job. I bit my tongue for a while to fit in and do my job, but eventually paid a price for it. I brought home my anger and emotions regarding work, which negatively affected my marriage. It also damaged other parts of my life, like the volunteer work I did. One person described me as having a "fiery edge." These two situations made it clear I needed to resign. However, the damage took a long time to reverse as I learned skills for processing work stress in a healthier way.

The truth of the matter is that the topic of sex, and even worse, sex itself, is a career killer. There is just not a place for the act, conversations, or even the undertones. Every employee, including yourself, should be able to go to work feeling as if it is a secure and safe environment. If they are talking about *you* at work but not about your *work*, you have a problem. Every action has a reaction. If you believe you're advancing your career because you're in an intimate relationship with your boss, that choice will come at a cost. There will be others. Some who are in leadership positions will lose respect for you. It can and will limit you.

Relationship versus Harassment. When you introduce sex into the workplace, you begin walking a very fine line. Think about a couple who begin a workplace romance. Things start off hot and heavy. Everyone is happy. Eventually, one of the two decides the relationship is a bad idea and decides to end it. The other participant isn't happy at all. He or she determines the relationship should continue and sends emails, texts, and makes constant inappropriate comments while at work. His or her counterpart has had enough and reports him or her to their superior. But it doesn't end there. On one fateful day, he or she decides to slap the other on the butt, thinking it to be a sign of affection. Multiple people witness this, and report him or her to the boss. He or she is then immediately fired.

My point is that what can start as a harmless relationship will eventually blur lines and boundaries and can escalate into something much more involved and serious. When a relationship ends, you will have to see your former significant other eight to ten hours per day and deal with the emotional baggage that goes along with that. Even if it doesn't result in harass-ment, it is not an easy scenario to navigate. This just shows that happy endings are extraordinarily rare.

Sleeping Your Way to the Top. Years after we hired a woman based on the recommendation of a client, I immediately noticed something was off, but couldn't figure out what it was. Follow-ing several awkward situations, I finally put the pieces together. Her life plan was to sleep her way up the ladder. That was her first problem. Her second problem was that happily married men and women in our company surrounded her. Quickly, she imploded and didn't retain her position for long. Only a few people would consider this as a reasonable route to the top, but it is a recipe for complete and utter disaster.

In addition to being immoral, and mentally and physically unhealthy, I've never seen this strategy work. Sex with cowork-ers will affect your job. Your time at work is for work. You want your coworkers to talk about the first class work you do, not your personal life. Time and energy are so precious, so be sure to spend them on healthy, productive goals.

Interoffice Gossip. We all love a good romance story, right? But when it comes to the drama at your workplace, avoid it. I've been guilty of this and regret it. However, I don't recall talking about others as a way of hurting them. That's true gos-sip, and you want to stay far away from it. If someone starts to gossip to you, shut it down. I've needed to talk out the issues I've had with people. While that's not wrong, I've failed by talking too much, talking to the wrong people, and hanging on to things too long. As I've become older, I've worked to hold my tongue. I take time to journal, focus on more healthy issues, and seek counsel outside of my work environment.

Talking about sex can be just as damaging to your potential growth as being the one within the relationship. Don't ever be the one spreading the gossip, especially regarding your cowork-ers. It is completely feasible to think that gossip will come back tenfold and result in false accusations about you and your true character.

Management's Hesitation to Promote You. Again, you have a problem if others are discussing your interactions with people in the workplace. The last thing you'll want is for your boss to factor in your personal life when considering a promotion. If your reputation is a problem, it represents a risk to *their* reputation in recommending that you move up in the company. It can work out for the best, but it usually doesn't. If you end up in a healthy relationship, that's great. In reality, it often doesn't happen though. Erin, from the TV show *The Office*, said it best when she stated, "The best thing about dating someone you work with is that if you break up, you still get to see them every day." This is awkward, if not a complete bar to your further growth and development within your company.

Sexual Addiction. Sexual addiction is a growing problem in our society. This compulsion, like drugs and alcohol, devastates millions of Americans. Once a young man in my office asked me if sexual addiction was even a real compulsion. I assured him it was. Like other addictions, people want to stop, but they just can't. Their obsession leads them down a path of increasingly dangerous behavior and toward disastrous consequences. One of the most successful mortgage brokers I've ever known had a huge house, beautiful family, and led his own firm. After attending the same real estate conference as he did one year, I went home. But he did not. He boarded a flight to Oklahoma, where he had scheduled a meeting with an underage girl. When he arrived, the "girl" turned out to be a police officer. His life began to fall apart. While awaiting trial, a couple of my close friends went to see him. One was a sex addict, so he understood the problem. They gave him excellent advice and a roadmap to recovery. He ignored them and pursued another relationship with an underage girl. Again, the "girl" turned out to be a cop. He's serving time in a federal prison. It's highly unlikely he'll ever come out. His addiction ruined not only his life, but his family.

Research Sexual Addiction. If it describes your behaviors, seek professional help so it does not derail your career. If not, be aware that you'll work with people who struggle with it. Consider that possibility before you feel complimented by someone pursuing you romantically. That person may simply be following a pattern of addiction that has held him captive for years. But it isn't always as serious as seeking a relationship with a child. You can safely assume that everything you do on your work computer can and will be seen by someone else.

The Ashley Madison hack in 2015 and subsequent names that were released damaged many careers. One example is a local government official who used his government email account to log on and look for love. Beyond the immorality of his act, the lack of wisdom raises concern about trusting someone who does something so foolish. Watch the evening news even once, and you'll hear about the trouble that emails can cause a person seeking to advance in a career. The unnecessary grief that accompanies choosing to indulge in inappropriate Internet activity comes with a strong bite. Resist and get help.

Many readers of this book probably don't feel it is an issue to visit one of *those* sites, but pornography has no place in a professional setting. Many employers are constantly monitoring their employees' computers to ensure work is getting done. Even one visit to a forbidden site can lead directly to termination. If you choose to visit these sites, do so in the privacy of your own home.

Sex is everywhere. You may feel it is following you around. But when it comes to your career, you now see the ways that sex can completely derail your growth. It is a bad idea to get intimately involved with your colleagues. This is not only a recipe for disaster, but even in the best of conditions, it will create distractions and prevent you from truly doing your best at work.

Even if you dodge the temptation of lust in the workplace, that doesn't mean you are out of the fire just yet. Be sensitive to your colleagues and always think about what you are saying to them. Even one inappropriate comment could lead to your immediate firing, or even something worse, like a lawsuit for sexual harassment. The bottom line is that you must remain hyperaware and do your best to separate yourself from the gossip and the conversations of which you need no part. This is a humongous career killer, but also one of the easiest landmines to completely avoid.

CHAPTER 4

Career Killer #3

GREED: MONEY *CAN* BE THE ROOT OF ALL KINDS OF EVIL

"Money, Money, Money, Money . . ."

—*O'Jays*

Jonathan Swift said, "A wise person should have money in their head, but not in their heart." We all love the idea of making money. Whether it be for financial independence, buying that fast car, big home, or taking a dream vacation—money matters. But there comes a point where the pursuit of money becomes remarkably unhealthy. Some money is great, but focusing only on money will cost you more than the money you might make.

So this brings us to the third career killer: greed.

Greed is the intense and selfish desire for something, especially wealth or power. The operative words in that definition are "intense" and "selfish." Neither of these words carry pure intentions and rarely work out to the advantage of the beholder. With that said, let's discuss how greed can bury your career.

Remember what Michael Douglas said in the movie *Wall Street*? "Greed is good." As much as I love that movie, I disagree with Mr. Douglas's character's assessment. "Greed ain't all that good for anyone." It leads to poor decisions, bad judgment, and generally speaking, negative consequences. I've always enjoyed the expression, "Pigs get fat. Hogs get slaughtered." Think about it. What does it mean to you? To me, it means you should make a lot of money and be successful, but leave something for others. Do not act or make a decision solely on your selfish desire to get as much as you can without thinking of the consequences. There's a difference between success and greed. We should all strive for success, but in a morally sound and high-character sort of way. Otherwise, we will start to get greedy.

As a business owner, I want Crossman & Company to grow, to be successful, and to make a lot of money. At the same time, I want the same for all the businesses with which we work. There is a big pie, and we can all enjoy a piece of it. I don't want to overpay my colleagues, but I do want them to be successful. The architects, landscapers, contractors, and retailers with whom I work can easily share in my success and financial gain. I never view it as a "me" versus "them" scenario. In the long run, if they are happy, they'll do good work for my clients and me.

It's really just a matter of morality. I want to run my company with high regard for everyone and be fair to others. Greed isn't about money. It's about gaining more at the expense of others. It is like a see-saw—when your side goes up, their side has to go down. I hate the thought of that. It's the attitude that I'm going to grow and forget everyone else—except me. That's a problem. I can't even recall the times I've seen businesses that grew bigger and wealthier but were eventually restricted and limited by their greedy behaviors.

Greed is not just limited to people who own a business. Greed creates just as many problems and issues among employees. Think about it. As an employee of any business, you have a responsibility to show up for work on time, complete your tasks, and do your best. If you are greedy, you may decide you want more time for yourself and then forgo some of your job requirements at the expense of your leadership. That impacts the entire team, not just you.

As a business owner or even an employee, choose an attitude of generosity and achievement instead of one surrounded with greed. Work at making a lot of money, but all the while ensure that the people around you also gain when you prosper. This makes sense, doesn't it? This goes beyond being a team player. Adopt the attitude that your success and growth go hand in hand with the success of your clients', customers', vendors', employees', and coworkers' success and growth. You do not want to be known for being greedy. That will quickly spread, and no one will want to work with you.

For example, one large company with which we did business does some things quite well. However, it struck me—and others in our company agreed—that they were quite greedy and pushy and were demanding too much from their colleagues and employees. After a period of consideration, we fired them because of this repeated and egregious behavior. They produced for us, but there had been a substantial cost associated with that production. It just didn't feel right.

After this, we contacted four major corporations with which we did business and let them know that we were severing our relationship with this company. One of our calls was to Florida State University. All four companies told me the same thing: "Way to go. Those people are terrible." Their consistent response fascinated me. This greedy company believed their decisions would generate more money. Over the long run, they didn't. The best and brightest talent repeatedly chose other companies and didn't recommend them. People quit looking for ways to do favors for them, because they didn't build the kind of relationships other companies do. We all sniffed out their practices and behaviors, and they lost a great opportunity over the long haul.

I'm a big believer in achievers—those successful people who take their skillset to the highest level. When I compare success to greed, there lies the difference: You can be very successful without taking advantage of someone else. As I have more influence and income, I want the same for everyone around me. When people are greedy, they want increased assets at others' expense. They don't care who they hurt or the carnage they leave. They only care about how much they get to eat, even if everyone else around them is starving and fighting over the scraps. An outlook seeking to gain at the expense of others is unhealthy and will backfire and cause even greater loss than if you just did the right thing.

Greed is everywhere, and many times we don't even know just how greedy people are. One of my favorite (and somewhat tongue in cheek) examples comes from the fast-food industry. I don't eat at McDonald's often, but I learned that a few years ago they removed the ever-popular double cheeseburger. Why did they do that? It wasn't cost-effective. Eventually, they brought it back but called it the McDouble. The difference? It was the same exact hamburger, with one less slice of cheese. This may seem like a silly example, but that single slice of cheese accounted for millions of dollars over the course of hamburger sales. This example of greed is not a true career killer, but McDonald's sells a lot less of these hamburgers now. This goes to show that greed comes in many shapes and colors, even square and orange. This is a small-scale example, and no one was desperately injured in the process. But there are many more real-life examples that occur almost every day.

Years ago, I mentored a young man who excelled in his career but really struggled in his personal life. I asked him, "What do you think the problem is?" He said, "I don't think my coworkers respect me." Years after this conversation, he's financially well off, but sadly, is even less respected in the industry. One of the main reasons is his insatiable greed. He only seemed to care about getting more for himself, and he failed to pay people internally and externally what would be considered an equal share.

The money he's made hasn't repaired the suffering in those other areas of his life. Why? He feeds a demon within himself that will never be satisfied and will always steal his peace. A story like his usually has an unhappy ending. When people are known for being greedy, they miss out on other opportunities. They don't see the value in every deal, they just focus on the personal and financial gain.

One guy used information he had acquired from a marketing colleague to try for a deal. He got it. But he didn't use his marketing colleague to work on that deal. He had simply *used* him for the information. Years later, he found out about a huge opportunity that he had missed the chance to work on. He found out the guy who was running the deal was in fact the guy he had used for his own gain. His greed had blocked him from another opportunity. The examples are endless. The most important thing to consider is that money is just one thing to gain from a deal or a business endeavor. There is always so much more at stake. As business leaders, we are always willing to celebrate healthy ambition. We all want to work with people who are dedicated, determined, and appreciate success. But those same people have to see the value in a win-win philosophy. I know people who have built million-dollar businesses from helping others. Their generosity and genuine caring for others unlocked doors that would have remained closed.

In short, don't be greedy. It is a true career killer. If you think you are greedy, then let's work to cure your ailment. The cure for greed is intentional thought about changing attitudes and behaviors. Make sure people you work with are properly paid and appreciated. Don't let *your* success come at the expense of anyone else.

Years ago, I read an excellent article in the book *The Achievers* on healthy and unhealthy motivators in leadership. Some unhealthy motivators are getting power when it's not needed, being popular, and trying to get credit for everything others have contributed to. Greed is an unhealthy way to lead; it's damaging and will result in a loss. If you are an employee, greed is the wrong way to develop and grow within your company. People can spot a team player a mile away. And they can spot a self-serving, righteous jerk ten miles away. The choice is yours. Who do you want to be?

We all want to succeed in our personal and professional lives. It doesn't happen overnight. But if you try to advance through greed, you might see some immediate progress, but that will eventually slow. Think of the greedy executive who embezzles funds. Where is he now? Likely in prison. Or the greedy employee who continuously throws his coworkers under the bus for personal gain. Where is he? Likely without a job or personal relationships. These are just two examples of how greed plays itself out in the workplace. Don't fall into either trap. You will get ahead if you work hard, are nice to people, and always do the right thing.

Avoid greed at all costs. Introspection is a good way to prevent it. No matter who you are or what you do, always take an objective look at your behaviors. Next, be open and ask someone you trust to share with you if they or any of your mutual colleagues perceive you to be greedy. If the seeds of greed are starting to sprout, follow the feedback you receive. You might even turn to a coach or trusted advisor to help you through these internal issues before they become external. Freeing yourself from greed is an internal process, though one we should all consider accepting and executing.

Greed comes in many shapes and sizes. Sometimes it can be masked by other actions. Though it sounds contradictory, some people can be very charitable but still greedy—meaning, their motivators for that generosity are recognition, for more opportunities to increase wealth by a show of generosity, as well as to feel superior to others. Getting away from this mindset requires a long process of evaluation and deliberately making value changes to how you act and why you do what you do.

I'd rather have less money and be much healthier and respected by my peers. I hope the same for you. There is no issue with personal gain and building great wealth. I want that for all of you. If you work hard, you deserve to enjoy the benefits from your work—but never at the expense of others. Mahatma Gandhi said, "Earth provides enough to satisfy every man's needs, but not every man's greed." We are in this together, so let's work to succeed side by side and hand in hand.

CHAPTER 5

Career Killer #4

TEMPERAMENT: NO ONE LIKES A HOTHEAD

> "He who keeps his cool best wins."
>
> —*Norman Cousins*

We all likely know one—that guy or girl who just can't seem to keep it together in moments of despair. They either have an anger issue or just flip out when they are stressed and frustrated. When they lose their cool, the result is a counterproductive and completely unnecessary behavior. They lash out, yell, scream, wave their hands in the air, or even worse. Why? No reason in particular. They just cannot maintain control because they're a hothead.

It's another big-time career killer.

The television show *The Office* is like therapy for me. It's even good in reruns. When Andy Bernard, AKA the Nard Dog, lost his temper and punched a hole in the wall, they sent him to anger management to solve this personal problem affecting his workplace decision making.

You may have heard of the book of Proverbs in the Old Testament. One of the oldest books ever written, it's thirty-one chapters of wisdom. If you read it at the rate of a chapter a day, you'll finish it in a month. Again and again, it warns not to associate with quick-tempered people. These are the type of people whose anger will eventually bring them to their knees. Just wait for it. No doubt, they will eventually succumb to a situation that triggers erratic behavior. Woodrow Wilson said it best: "One cool judgment is worth a thousand hasty counsels. The thing to do is to supply light and not heat." I would suggest you subscribe to that train of thought. Stay cool, remain calm, and think before you act.

A VERY HARMFUL, IMMATURE TRAIT

Hotheads instantly take offense, grow angry, and react defensively. On most occasions, their behavior isn't even proportionate to the scenario. Most of the time, they are operating from a point of overkill. You've probably met people with a quick, negative response to most any situation. When I was younger, I mistakenly thought these guys were tough. They could take out anyone and were willing to do so at the drop of a hat. But the older I get, the more I realize the truth in those proverbs. Hotheadedness is a destructive, immature trait, not something to be celebrated and respected.

These people are like children without self-control. Their default decision making is to grab things and display impulsive, reactive behavior. When you're selecting business relationships, evaluate who you associate with, why you connect with them, and use caution with hot-tempered ones. Most people will tell you that Mike Tyson is one of the greatest boxers of all time. He was a combination of sheer force and destructive punching ability. But he was also a hothead. And when he fought Evander Holyfield, it was remarkably obvious. I am sure we all remember the fight when Tyson bit off a piece of Holyfield's ear.

In multiple interviews, Tyson said he had been frustrated, annoyed, and had acted out. He admits he made a mistake. For a boxer who lived in the limelight and was considered one of the best of all time, many people remember him for this hotheaded decision. Now, the writing is always on the wall. Tyson has always been an impulsive and quick-to-react kind of guy. That is partly why he was such a great boxer. But in that moment in Las Vegas, under the lights, with millions of people watching, Tyson let his hotheaded nature get the best of him. From a boxing standpoint, he was never the same again.

That is the risk of being a hothead. You allow your emotions, not your brain, to inform your actions. Hotheads act without thought and pay a grave price later. Awhile back, I received a call from one of the best guys I've ever known and one of the most successful in the nation. He shared with me that there was a lot of turmoil within the big national company where he worked. After leaving the office one day, he arrived at home and received a FedEx envelope. It contained his termination letter. Right after he was fired, they even locked the office down and closed it the next day. He told me what happened and asked what I thought was going on. I was quick to share with him, "You've got a bit of a temper problem." That was an understatement. "And you talk about all the guns you own." Later, he found out that they let him go in that manner to avoid a potentially dangerous situation.

He was devastated. But it turned out to be the best thing that ever happened to him. It made him assess the situation and seek help. There are examples everywhere. One of the worst examples I know involved a hotheaded guy who worked in my office building, but not directly with me. One day he claimed a desk that one of my employees was using. When I asked him why, he denied the action. Then his assistant called him out as a liar in front of me. I returned an hour later to handle the situation. When I did, he exploded. He was a much bigger guy than me. He grabbed something on the desk, slammed it down, then thrust it toward me saying, "Here's your rattle, baby!"

I thought, *This guy is going to swing at me. He's going to punch me in an office building, in a professional environment.* I walked away and called the national human resources (HR) department. They came and investigated the situation, speaking to everyone about the encounter. Eventually, they concluded the hothead was at fault and acted without provocation. He even had the nerve to claim he did it because I acted insubordinate.

Although we were both partners, I said, "That can't be the case because I don't report to him." Their solution: We should stay away from each other. I said, "How? We work in the same building. Aren't you going to set up a meeting to work out some kind of reconciliation?" They indicated they would not and repeated the directive to stay away from him. That was a moment of clarity. He made the company a lot of money, so they didn't want to risk losing him—or me—but they also didn't want to stir things up. Ultimately, he was the real victim. Despite his productivity, no one cared enough about him to help him deal with his demons.

Later on, I found out his twenty-fifth anniversary with the company was approaching and called corporate headquarters. "It's his twenty-fifth anniversary. Shouldn't we have some kind of party for him?" Even though I didn't like him and felt like he was inches away from hitting me on that day, I believed coordinating a celebration was the right thing to do. They agreed. So I talked to the office manager, the managing director, his assistant, and the HR coordinator. Four for four, they all said, "No way." I can't think of a sadder situation than a senior executive who has worked twenty-five years at one company but who doesn't have even one person in his corner. There are certainly better career achievements than to work for decades and never develop any relationships. But that is what happens to hotheads. They are respected out of fear, not out of friendship.

DANGER, DANGER

Hotheads aren't just a danger to the workplace, they are a danger to everyone. Have you been reading the paper or watching the news lately? If so, I am willing to bet you have heard the story of a boyfriend or husband killing his wife in a fit of rage. They refer to it as domestic violence, and the rate of these incidents is growing with alarming speed. They happen every day. When a relationship flounders or dissolves, love and commitments, whether personal or business, can turn into resentment and anger. That anger can fester and grow and eventually lead to a tragic incident that was completely avoidable. Being a hothead isn't just a career killer, it can be a real killer.

Think it couldn't happen to you? Assess how your partner or loved one deals with difficult situations. Does he or she yell, throw things, hit things, or even put his or her hands on you? If so, the writing is on the wall. There is absolutely an anger issue that needs to be addressed.

But it doesn't stop there. We are seeing a growing number of road-rage incidents across the United States. It feels like it's more and more common to hear of a roadside incident that resulted in serious injury. Most times it starts with a verbal or nonverbal gesture, a traffic accident, or just beeping your horn or cutting people off. The other driver then grossly overreacts, even getting out of his or her car to confront you. I always subscribe to the notion that if you want to cut me off, beep your horn, or wave with just one finger, then so be it. It is not worth my safety to respond. You just never know when the other driver has a gun in his glove compartment.

I'm sharing these stories with you to help you avoid the hotheads. To some degree, you can work to diffuse difficult scenarios and ensure they do not escalate to become something much more serious. Hotheads hide everywhere, and you may not know someone has anger issues until it is too late. So do your best to avoid conflict, and walk away from risky situations.

CHOOSE CAREFULLY

Be very careful with whom you associate. If a coworker has an anger issue, you might find yourself in the crossfire. He or she may not take his or her anger out on you, but that doesn't mean it couldn't impact you or your job. There is an old saying out there: "When you hang out with dogs, you catch fleas." Always consider who you keep as your company.

Choose your partners and associates wisely. Be careful about who you work for, who you work with, and who you keep in your inner circle, as each of these people will help to define you. Use your intelligence and people skills to decide the best fit for you when making meaningful commitments. Caution doesn't mean that you have to kick them out of your life completely, but it makes sense to limit the connection you have with certain people.

We had a client who worked with our Orlando and Miami offices. He was closer to me than anyone else in the company, so it was no surprise he called me when he was struggling with our Miami office. In turn, I called the Miami team on his behalf.

The team leader there almost immediately raised his voice. "We don't need people from Orlando telling us how to do our jobs!" Calmly, I replied that *clearly* he did because of this client's concerns. He punched the desk near the speakerphone so loudly, I could hear the thud. Then he hung up on me. His volatile behavior prompted me to contact human resources and recommend they check on him. At the time, he was being considered for a major promotion that I was unaware of, and because of his outburst, he was removed from consideration. One outburst led to a series of unintended consequences. But that is the problem for most hotheads: They do not consider the consequences before they act. If they did, they wouldn't be hotheads.

We all have our triggers—those things that upset us and infuse an enormous amount of emotion into our hearts and minds. That is normal, and most people would refer to that as "life." But how we respond to these situations is what separates us from one another. Choose calm, choose thoughtful, and choose to walk away. No workplace situation is worth a physical or anger-driven confrontation. Even if you are completely and utterly in the right, your hotheaded response will make you wrong.

No one likes a hothead. They seemed like the cool guys or gals in high school, but losing your cool isn't cool at all. Dealing with situations with physical force or anger isn't cool either. In fact, that borders on criminal behavior. But more than anything, it is a quick way to get yourself fired, or at least lose the support of your colleagues and superiors. It's even worse if you are in a leadership role. You should be an example to your employees.

If you resort to anger and yelling to handle situations, don't be surprised if your team does the same. An uncontrolled temper not only affects the natural camaraderie of the workplace but negatively hinders the concentration and enthusiasm critical to productive work.

Chinese philosopher Lao Tzu said, "The best fighter is never angry." There is great value in this statement. Anger clouds your judgment and makes you act out of something other than a thoughtful and strong place. Being a hothead is a surefire way to kill your career. So take the time to address your underlying anger issues, if they exist, and work to remain calm, cool, and collected as you navigate your personal and professional life.

CHAPTER 6

Career Killer #5

PRIDE: HUMILITY ALWAYS WINS OUT

"It was pride that changed angels into devils;
it is humility that makes men as angels."

—*Saint Augustine*

We should all be proud of who we are and what we do. Pride is a characteristic trait most leaders, employers, friends, and colleagues certainly covet. I like to surround myself with people who take pride in their work, their character, and their morals. Pride is extremely important. Most people lacking it do not go far in life. But like icing on a cake, and most other things in life, too much pride is not necessarily a good thing. To that end, the final career killer we'll discuss is having too much pride in your personal or professional life.

Beth Azor, president of Azor Advisory Services, a commercial real estate advisory and investment firm based in Southeast Florida, shared with me, "One of the most frustrating observations I see when mentoring recent graduates is their inability to be curious and ask questions. I see this more with young men than young women. I believe that young men feel that if they ask questions, it shows that they do not know everything. That is a place they don't want to be. Remember, bosses don't expect new graduates to know everything. This is likely a pride thing, an arrogance thing, or maybe just insecurity! Get humble, people! Admit you are new, inexperienced, and want to learn! Be teachable! That's what leads to success! Mentors want to advise young professionals who are eager to learn. If you present yourself like you already know it all, then most mentors will scratch their head. Ask questions and be curious."

Pride is a dangerous, powerful trait that can often lead to the loss of business, the loss of excellent employees, and the loss of business associates. At one time, we had a woman in our office who did accounting and human resource work. A bright, hard-working employee, she aspired to grow with our company and was on target to achieve her goals. As a pillar of our company, we believe that leading equates to taking care of other people. It is not always easy to do that, but we require it. It calls for sacrifice and often putting other peoples' needs above your own. But those who succeed are willing to do just that. Because of her potential, I put her in charge of our company's new website and explained to her that it was an important job. It involved interaction with the experts in our leasing, sales, and marketing departments. While the marketing department is brilliant in accomplishing its goals, they tend to be very gregarious and sometimes unfocused, and they have proclaimed themselves as terrible with deadlines. For instance, if you tell them you need to hear back from them by noon the next day, you might as well put your hands together and pray they have nothing else on their plate. As you can imagine, their lack of prompt responses immensely frustrated this employee.

I arrived at work one Friday morning, excited to see our new website a few hours before its scheduled launch. So I powered up my laptop and clicked on our hyperlink. Surprise: The website was already live. I'm the president of the company, and my team hadn't even let me know it was ready. It had a ton of typos and other mistakes. This was not cool. I sent an email to the employee who had been charged with working on the project and to her boss, asking, "What's up with the website? This is a real problem for me."

That was when I found out the employee charged with overseeing the website had taken a personal day. She'd launched the website on a Thursday and taken a personal day on Friday without notifying anyone. So I sent her another email, which was likely a little bit harsher in tone. I wanted her to address the problem and fix these issues. Besides, our website was likely the first thing many potential clients would see. I didn't hear back from her. But after hours, her boss called me and told me she had come in after work to meet with him. He shared with me that she had resigned by saying, "I'm fed up. I'm not working with those salespeople. I'm done."

This upset me. Why? We had planned to fire her boss and offer her a big promotion and build the company around her in a way. The first hurdle she had to clear was reimagining our website. We wanted to see how she would handle it, and she failed miserably.

As we began to dive deeper into the communication, or lack thereof, we learned that her pride had prevented her from accomplishing this task. She wasn't open, accepting, and patient with her team. She barely communicated with others. She didn't set out a schedule and game plan and simply ran this project by the seat of her pants. She was so confident and so prideful that she didn't even edit the copy before she posted it on our website. Had she thought things out and worked them through, she would have been promoted and received a pay raise. Her pride had kept her from moving forward. Too bad, but not surprising.

Strike 1: *She thought she knew it all.*
Strike 2: *She was unwilling to work with others.*
Strike 3: *She didn't even review her work.*

One strike would have been enough, but she whiffed three times. That is pride at its finest. Pride can be defined as "a feeling or deep pleasure or satisfaction derived from one's own achievements, the achievements of those with whom one is closely associated, or from qualities or possessions that are widely admired." This sounds like a positive definition, right? Well, pride must be balanced with humility. Otherwise, it can become an unwanted trait rather than a coveted one.

At some point, we must face our pride and let it go. Much of it is tied to our abilities, yet, over time, those abilities can change. Prideful people often overvalue their own abilities and see themselves different than the world may view them. Consider the following examples: Those with great athletic achievement reach a day when their prized ability begins to fade. Denial only lasts so long, then reality sets in. Highly intelligent individuals may either quietly or overtly brag about their mental acuity and accumulated knowledge. But a day comes when that quick mind will slow and knowledge will begin to drift away. Highly attractive men and women often use this quality throughout their lives, but despite cosmetics and surgery, these externals diminish in time.

The physical and mental peaks we enjoy will eventually decline, so you must embrace the change that life offers. When we acknowledge that our time in the sun has passed, then we can admit it's someone else's turn. Living with comfort about each stage of life means there's a season to stand on the stage and receive recognition and a time to be the audience for others. I've found that the more I embrace things I don't do well, the healthier I get. I'm more at peace with myself and more satisfied with my life.

Over time, I have recognized that substantial pride can have two remarkably negative effects:

1. It makes you think you know and can do everything on your own.
2. It prevents you from adjusting to the changing environment of your life.
   - *We are all familiar with the guy who is unwilling to ask for directions when he is lost.*
   - *Or your friend who insists on completing that home improvement project without the help of a more experienced contractor.*
   - *Maybe that work colleague who stays at work until late at night, unable to enjoy dinner with her family because she has to finish that project on her own.*

- *Or that coworker who doesn't review his or her work regularly because he or she is confident she nailed it the first time.*

These are all examples of how pride can lead you down a path you don't want to journey on. History is riddled with examples of scholars, academics, and leading thinkers whose pride led to their great demise. When describing pride, Dr. Steven Aicinena says, "In truth, pride is double-edged: destructive and ludicrous in the wrong place and the wrong proportions, but heroic and admirable in the right ones."

As a sports fan, you notice pride can often be a career killer. Consider modern-day baseball. Can you think of just a few examples of professional baseball players who turned to performance-enhancing drugs simply to maintain their high level of athletic ability? They were eventually caught, and many of them were banned from playing the sport they loved. Maybe it was their competitive spirit or bad judgment that led to the use of these banned substances. But pride played an important role too. They just couldn't handle their diminished skillset, so they risked their legacy and morals to compete.

The inability of many to admit their mistakes or their need to get better proves that pride often correlates to terrible judgment. The most talented and successful people I meet are the least frightened because they've survived tough times. Getting through those periods taught them how fragile any success is and how quickly it can change. Pride should always be balanced; it is possible to have too much of it.

Our country experienced an extraordinary recession throughout the real estate market from 2007–2009. During that time, I knew at least five successful people who committed suicide. I believe all of them would have survived the downturn, but their pride blinded them and they could only see suicide as an option. We all know it wasn't. Once driving luxury sedans and living in a huge house, they were struggling to pay bills and stay ahead. Pride took over, and they took their own lives.

It's tragic that people worked hard for years to build successful careers, only to end them with ego and self-righteousness. I've seen people who've made millions of dollars lose millions of dollars. It's not because they were stupid, but their egos were so big they couldn't admit they had made mistakes or were wrong in the first place. Don't let your ego get in the way. It's okay to be corrected or disciplined. Own up to flaws in decisions and errors in judgment. Communicate. Be open about situations; no one is expected to be perfect. The solution may be right at your fingertips if someone else knows what you're struggling with. You *can* grow through your challenges.

Pride is an important quality to possess, but always balance it with a humble approach to your personal and professional life. Too much pride will inevitably lead you to closed doors rather than open ones. I once heard the following quote: "Pride will be the longest distance between two people." Those words embody just how damaging pride can be. Your pride should motivate you to do great work, build strong friendships, and pay attention to the details in your life. Use it for good, and don't let it overcome your sensibilities and kill your career.

PART III

The Career Builders

So far, we have focused on the missteps that can truly kill a career. But that's enough about the negative. The remainder of our focus will be on those exciting steps you can take to build your career. Most of us are not going to succumb to alcohol, drugs, dishonesty, pride, or our emotions. We are going to put our heads down, work hard, and make the decisions that will help us progress through the layers of the professional world. These are critical to long-term success, because economies ebb and flow and layoffs happen, even to top performers.

The job market is a fiercely competitive arena, and you must use every resource and advantage to remain light-years ahead of the competition. As students of our profession, we should always diligently work to learn and improve. The second you accept the status quo will be the beginning of the end. Don't think for even one second that your boss or leadership will acknowledge that average is good enough.

Remember that a career isn't the same as a job. A friend of mine likes to say that a career is something you think about when you're brushing your teeth. It's part of you. If you've found your career and want to invest your fullest capabilities, the forthcoming chapters are for you.

CHAPTER 7

Career Builder #1

MENTORS: IT TAKES A VILLAGE TO SUCCEED

"A mentor is someone who allows you
to see the hope inside yourself."

—*Oprah Winfrey*

Benjamin Franklin said, "Tell me and I forget, teach me and I may remember, involve me and I learn." The idea of mentorship has been around since the beginning of time. Think of every great athlete, entertainer, coach, CEO, executive, president, and leader. Every one of these remarkable individuals had people help them along the way. They were once the students, and they have now respectively transformed into the leading teachers. At the end of the day, no one does it alone. When it comes to building a professional career, it is crucial to surround yourself with the trailblazers and pioneers who have walked the difficult path before you. These key motivators will act like bright lanterns, guiding you along the way. There is no better measurement of success than those with whom you surround yourself.

Remember Mr. Miyagi from the movie *The Karate Kid*? To achieve progress and skill, he mentored through time, instruction, and correction. But the development of "Daniel-*san*" was always the pivotal part of the story. We watched this young man with little discipline and drive turn into a dedicated and determined martial artist. Against all odds, Daniel-*san* transformed into a champion, defeating the Cobra Kai. Now I know this is just Hollywood, but it offers an important point for us all. That is, proper mentoring is an extremely valuable resource and tool to introduce into your own life. As a young professional, you'll find a great need for people to help you overcome obstacles and challenges.

As you begin your career, latch on to the game changers who can become the difference makers within your own life. To find a good mentoring match, start by seeking healthy relationships. Most people think of mentorship as a one-way street. That is, the mentor takes the mentee under his or her wing and gives the necessary time, effort, and attention to develop that young guy or gal. However, I want you to not only value the importance of a mentor, but also to recognize that it is a two-way street and you have your own set of responsibilities in the relationship as well.

If you want someone's help, find a way to serve that person too. Practice give and take. What can you offer to your mentor? Technology know-how? Time? Don't be a charity case. Be eager to learn, but remain eager to also give back. Be committed to your mentor's organization, business, or personal needs. These people know others who can help your career and will dedicate more time to your relationship if they recognize that they are benefiting not just from helping you, but in some other fashion too.

To gain the most from a mentoring relationship, let your energy flow back to your mentor from your unique background and great attitude. Creatively consider how to enhance your mentor's life with your own skills and abilities. Many mentoring situations flow naturally out of a work environment and take place between a manager and more experienced employee. The time you spend together may vary from a few days to a few months, depending on the knowledge and skill being transferred from one to another. The structure may be as simple as enhancing your knowledge or perfecting your skills. Here are some steps you can take as a mentee to create the healthiest relationship for your mentor:

- Avoid the trap of neediness through active, regular gratitude. Always remind your mentor just how appreciative you are of his or her efforts. A simple handwritten thank you card or thoughtful gift can easily do the trick.
- Offset the multitude of complaints leaders receive with a genuine compliment. "Hey I think you're doing a great job" goes a long way. Better yet, compliment them on something specific. Take it even one step further and post a good review on Yelp or encourage them on Facebook.
- Offer your time, youthful energy, and strength. Become aware of events the leaders and CEOs participate in, and offer your assistance for even mundane tasks. If you don't know of anything, ask, "You've been helping me. What can I do to help you?"
- Share in your success. Most mentors will tell you they dedicate time and effort to others because they want to share in the success of their mentees. Allow them to do just that. Take any opportunity you can to invite your mentor into your personal and professional life and show them how their efforts are truly paying off.

A guy I barely knew emailed me. He wrote: "John, you seem to be doing a lot to help people. Can I come to your house and cut your grass? Or do something else to help you?" While I appreciated his offer, I didn't need him to cut my lawn, but I loved his attitude and I ended up hiring him. His very successful career with us started when he tried to give back, simply because I had mentored him. So listen: Identify needs and show up or offer a kind word. Rarely is help about money; it's more often about being available and willing to be there for others.

PICKING YOUR MENTOR

As we begin to better understand the scope of a positive mentoring relationship, we can then turn our attention to finding a great mentor. To begin, you must have the attitude of gratitude. One of the biggest mistakes people make is to say, "I'm looking to build relationships" when they're not. What they really want is charity, because if they don't get what they want, then they are gone. In every arena of life, you'll meet key people who are passionate about helping others. They'll be eager to help you, so build good business relationships by making sure you're giving back in various ways. Some of the best places to look for mentors include:

- College
- Graduate School
- Your Job
- Your Friends
- Through LinkedIn, Facebook, and Other Social Media Sites
- Former Educators
- Professional Networking Groups
- Mastermind Groups
- Family Members
- Friends of Your Family

And many more . . .

Mentors are everywhere. I challenge you to complete even one week without meeting or engaging with someone you feel could help you throughout the course of your journey. Always keep your antenna up—remain aware and keep your eyes open. While mentors are all over the place, however, not every mentor will be the right fit for you. You must find the correct match for your needs and personality. Take the following steps to accomplish this:

1. *Identify Your Needs.* To choose the right mentor, consider the areas in which you need help. If you are a strong marketer but lack leadership skills, perhaps you should turn to a high-end executive who is responsible for leading many employees. As you identify your personal strengths and weaknesses, choose a mentor who can act as an accelerator, helping you to groom extremely well-considered and necessary skills.
2. *Stand Out and Ask.* If you want great mentorship, speak up and ask for it. I once asked some successful CEOs this:

"If you had a student from your alma mater who contacted you and said, 'I'd like to come and volunteer for a day at your company, just to be around you, get coffee, whatever you need,' would you agree to it?" One hundred percent said they would. Then I asked, "How many students have ever asked you that?" None had that experience. Look for people you admire, and then ask them if you can volunteer and help them in any way. Pour this kind of spirit into your relationships. You don't want to spend your life like a child who has his hand out. Instead, be an adult and cultivate healthy relationships in which you give and receive.

3. *Excel as a Potential Mentor.* Mentors want to invest time in those they believe will succeed. Aim to stand out in school and in all your endeavors. We all want to hitch our wagon to a true winner. It really is not enough that you simply want the help. It is also extremely important to show your potential mentor that you really mean business. Past performance can predict future results. Show your mentors you are ready not only to rise to the occasion but also to use your new-founded resources to do great things.

Each of these concerted efforts will help you locate and then secure a strong mentor.

A leading real estate executive once told me, "Forget about the deals. Forget about the numbers. Pick five people you can pour your life into." I find that to be extremely meaningful guidance. As a mentee, recognize that professionals want to help you. Many of them perceive mentorship as a basic human function, and they are chomping at the bit to find a young student of the game who they can impact and leave a lasting impression on.

FIND A WAY TO GIVE BACK

We touched on it earlier in the chapter, but mentorship is a two-way street. When you think about having a mentor, you likely begin your search by looking for someone who is older and more experienced than you. Now, I'll challenge you with this question: *What are you giving back?* If they agree to help you, what do they get from you? When you're trying to get a mentor, think of ways to assist him or her.

Years ago, a young man came to see me who was deciding whether to attend graduate school at the University of Florida. I met with him for a little while, but I couldn't stay very long because my family and I were moving to a new home that weekend. Later that day, he emailed me. He wrote, "Mr. Crossman, thanks for meeting with me. You said you're moving this weekend. Do you need any help?"

I thought, *Wow. This kid's impressive.*

That's Whitaker. I declined his move-in offer, but I went on to hire him, and he has enjoyed an extremely successful career. But what I saw in him in those first moments was a young man who was asking me for something but at the same time was trying like crazy to give me something in return. And he did so in a completely genuine way. Needless to say, he left a great first impression.

Another example is a guy I met through church, who later emailed me this: "John, you do all these things to help people. I want to do something to help you. Can I cut your grass?" I read those words and said, "Who is this guy?" Although I didn't know him at the time, we eventually hired Andy Lively to act as HR director of our company. We loved his spirit and willingness to do anything to get the job done, even cutting my grass.

So whoever your mentors are, let your life and your efforts focus on them. Give them time and offer to come by their office, bring them lunch, or grab them a coffee. Send them links to interesting articles, drop them a line when their favorite sports team gets the W, and continue to celebrate their victories as they celebrate your own.

Oftentimes, mentorship is a forgotten team game. It takes a village to create a great business, but it starts with the people.

Those people need support, love, and care. If you're a business leader, work hard to create a mentorship program within your organization. The little amount of time you invest into building this structure will pay off greatly. If you are a young professional, determine those people who are best positioned to serve you in a meaningful way and to act as your mentors. The need for mentorship may never change. Don't think just because you are a seasoned vet that you don't need others' advice and guidance. We are all in this together, and we will need to constantly support one another and move the needle along the way.

Mentorship is the first career builder. Over the course of my entire career, I have watched young men and women latch on to more experienced and well-trained individuals. They then reach their goals and targets much sooner than their colleagues who attempt to navigate the terrain on their own. We all need the map and compass. That is what mentorship provides. Early in your career, analyze your needs and find those people who can help you evolve.

CHAPTER 8

Career Builder #2

RELATIONSHIPS: FAMILY AND FRIENDS LEAD THE CHARGE

"Never above you. Never below you. Always beside you."
—*Walter Winchell*

Pop singer Kelly Clarkson said, "My friends and family are my support system. They tell me what I need to hear, not what I want to hear and they are there for me in the good and bad times. Without them I have no idea where I would be and I know that their love for me is what's keeping my head above the water." It is simply impossible to navigate this funny thing called life alone. From birth, we are surrounded by family members working to help us understand and relate to our lives. Then we go to school and meet other people with whom we constantly interact. These become our friends, and we develop with them. We maintain these relationships, and they often grow into alliances with people with whom we regularly choose to connect. While friends and family become the cornerstones of our lives, we also relate and intermingle with thousands of acquaintances along the way. These are the people who come and go but have some minimal impact on our journey. Looking at your life, think about your own friends, family, and acquaintances. You simply couldn't exist without these fundamental connections.

Over time, you likely find that some of these relationships grow and strengthen while others fizzle out and you lose track of people. That is normal. Your friends in elementary school may be quite different than those in college. Those in college may be substantially dissimilar to those you maintain into your adulthood. But one thing I can tell you is that relationships matter, and they influence your career, whether you allow them to or not. Choosing the right kinds of relationships is integral to not only living a happy life, but also building a successful career. As we just touched on, there are three levels of relationships we should consider. Each of these plays a pivotal role within our lives and impacts them in varying degrees. They include:

1. Acquaintances
2. Friends
3. Family

Let's unpack each one.

ACQUAINTANCES

Acquaintances are people you've just met or only slightly know or maintain relationships with. They are the arm-length friends or colleagues. Most of your time with your acquaintances is spent in small talk, short exchanges, and conversations with little substance. They are often one-off and could be people you see regularly where you shop or in large organizations where you know them only superficially but exchange pleasant greetings. Our connections with them are brief. You'd be unlikely to know their phone number, Facebook connections, family, or even outside interests.

Acquaintances have the least amount of impact on your life. They come and go. But that doesn't mean they can't affect you over time. As you decide with whom you'll interact, don't overlook the people you encounter daily, though at a distance. Even your acquaintances can make a real difference in the success or failures of your career.

Attention to details is extremely important to your overall success, and the acquaintances are in the details. If life is a game of inches, these are where we find the inches. Maybe it is a team member who has a small responsibility on a large project, or the owner of a local baking business creating a cake to celebrate the birthday of an important colleague, or your head of human resources who you don't know well but rely on for hiring and firing advice. Each of these people plays a small role in your life but can make a difference if they drop the ball or don't get the job done. This is why I always say that you must surround yourself with driven, motivated, and honest people. Whether we are talking about your husband, wife, best friend, or just an acquaintance, they all matter. So don't forget about the little guys and always work to choose the right people for your life, even if you don't think they'll have a lasting impact. You just never know.

FRIENDS

The second category of relationships is your friends. The philosopher Mencius said, "Friends are the siblings God never gave us." Friends carry remarkable importance regarding the overall direction of your life. They'll be the ones standing by your side through good times and bad. They will also shape much of your behavior and certainly impact your decision making. As I speak to young men and women, I always stress the importance of surrounding yourself with people who make you a better person. Most of us have heard of the concept that we can often determine our success by looking at the five to ten people with whom we are closest. If they are successful, we will probably follow suit. If they are troublemakers and maintain low morals and character, then we'd be challenged not to have similar issues.

I always think of saying, "Hang out with dogs and you'll catch fleas." As I've grown and matured, I have considered and adjusted my friendships accordingly. That has made a tremendous difference in my development and success. Good friends support you, understand you, and do not judge you, but they also are willing to stand by your side and support you when the going gets tough. We all need that love and attention, because in the end, no one can do it alone.

Don't ever underestimate the power of a close friend. And remember that you can have different groups of friends. You might have a few friends you turn to during hard personal times, while a separate set helps you with professional advice. Some friends may help you decompress by regularly going to the movies or working out with you, while with others you achieve the same ends by enjoying a good meal or a cup of coffee with them. Some friends are good for certain opportunities, but not others. You might have a friend you love to travel with but would never take career advice from. That's fine. Overall, surround yourself with positive people, but allow them to play many roles or just one. Everyone can have a purpose, and that purpose can absolutely be singular in nature.

What defines friendship is encouragement. The TV show *Friends*, for example, could have been called *Encouragement*, because each character worked to help one another. In the end, that's what friends do. Think about Facebook friends who wish each other happy birthday and write positive posts to encourage each other, especially in times of need. Friendship has no specific box in which it may fit—it is different things to different people. However, if you want to progress in your career, you need a strong support system willing to stand by your side and to expect great things from you. That is the meaning of true friendship.

FAMILY

Before her tragic passing, Princess Diana said, "Family is the most important thing in the world." It is also one of the most important career builders around. Think about it. From the moment you enter this world, it is your family that teaches you how to understand and interact with the world around you. As you grow and develop, it is your parents, your brothers, and your sisters who shape you . . . who nurture you. Many of your strengths and even your weaknesses can likely be attributed to your family. If you are a great athlete, it's in part because your dad pushed you in the backyard every day. If you are an artist, it is likely because your mom laid the groundwork for a creative and engaging environment filled with wonder. And as you grow and develop, it is your family that stands next to you along the way.

We've all heard the saying, "Don't forget where you came from." When it comes to succeeding in your chosen profession, this rings extraordinarily true. Families come in many shapes and sizes. There is really no one size fits all. For example, I have a stepbrother who's an editor in Hollywood, where he's worked on popular shows like *The Bachelor* and *Duets*. He's won an Emmy, and I think that's funny and extremely weird. My dad was a pastor and very active in the Civil Rights Movement. By contrast, my brother and I work in real estate. And while we didn't follow in our father's footsteps, the invaluable lessons we learned from him helped shape our daily behaviors and practices.

For example, my father instilled hard work, morals, character, and a certain level of humanity in me. I inject all these wonderful skills into my own real estate company. I expect my employees and senior leadership to be caring, fair, honest, and thoughtful to our team. That came directly from my father, so it is important to note that whatever you choose to do, your upbringing and your family will shape how you interact with others in your career. Every family has a variety of personalities, interests, strengths, and achievements. They trickle down to you, eventually shaping your world.

While friends are extremely important, it is your family that can often offer the tough love and honesty that others might not feel comfortable contributing. At times, friends may fall short of that. And to succeed, sometimes you need complete and honest feedback. True, friends will encourage you and say nice things, but they won't necessarily say, for example, "You have food in your teeth" or "Your zipper's down." They're even less likely to say, "You drink too much," or "You get angry too fast," or "You need to go to counseling." That doesn't happen naturally. People don't instantly get intimate enough with you to speak to you in that personal, detailed way.

Surround yourself with your family. They may drive you crazy at times, but outside of a dog (which most people consider to be family), there are no other people who will offer you the unconditional love that your family can. You'll need them through thick and thin, and much of your success (or challenge) in life can be directly attributed to them.

Acquaintances, friends, and family—they all touch our lives to varying degrees and shape us in one form or another. Survey those people with whom you surround yourself, and work to ensure that you choose the right people to help support your personal and professional endeavors.

CHOOSE WISELY

Most of us simply want a group of people who keep us balanced and push us to become the best version of ourselves. Life is just so much better when people who care surround us. But you must choose wisely and consider those people you invite in. How do you choose positive relationships that support you?

Trust comes first. Your interactions and observations lead you to believe these individuals are open, considerate, and reliable. You observe fairness in their actions and attitudes toward others and decide that they're worthy of your trust.

Next, you begin to spend more time with those people. Your initial trust grows as you get to know them better and engage in more conversations at work or outside of work. This interaction reinforces your comfort level.

As a result of trust and time, you move to the third level, which is an intellectual and emotional connection. At that time, you likely realize you can express your opinions without repercussions. You become willing not only to voice dissenting opinions but also to hear them.

You arrive in these relationships by seeking them, by being open to them, by talking through things, and by desiring them. This can be hard because openness with others can mean exposure to painful comments. When it comes to love, it can mean heartbreak and extremely personal challenges. However, when people grow close to one another, difficult conversations come about in the context of genuine concern. And love gained is worth the risk of love lost. Everyone has emotional wounds, things that they're working on, or things that they've stuffed away and haven't wanted to work on. But if you wisely choose your acquaintances, your friends, and to a degree, your family, then you'll find the support you need to succeed.

SUCCESS IS BEING A GOOD FRIEND

We are all looking for good friends, but we all have a responsibility to be a good friend as well. We have all heard the saying that we get what we give. When it comes to relationships, no statement is more accurate than that. Being a friend is not always easy. It is not always popular. At times, it can be downright difficult.

A guy once came up to me at a conference and said, "You know that woman who used to work with you?"

I said, "Sure."

"You know she's married, and she's having an affair with that guy who used to work with you?"

I said, "No way." He nodded his head. "Yeah, absolutely. That's happening."

It really bothered me. I didn't work with him anymore, but this news hurt me and made me sad. So I emailed my former female coworker. "Hey, what's going on with you and this guy? What's the deal?"

She responded, "How dare you?" She was mad.

I emailed her back. "Look, my goal isn't to be your friend. My goal is to be your brother. I care enough about you to risk you hating me to make you aware that people know."

If somebody was ever saying those things about me, I would absolutely want to know. I'd want that rooted out immediately.

Six months later, she called me. "Can I come see you?"

She came. She cried, admitted that she was having an affair, and she was sorry. But that's not the point of the story. Here's the point: From the moment I found out she was having an affair, twenty other people shared the same story with me. Everybody knew. But she said that I was the only one who called her out on it. Best friends who sat next to her at work didn't. They all knew, but none of them talked to her about it. In sharing this information with her, my goal wasn't to be popular. Rather, my goal was to care for her and be a good friend.

So as a friend, you must be conscious and thoughtful. You'll be a failure as a friend if you simply tell others they are great and don't need to change. You need people who love you enough to trust you, make time for you, and occasionally tell you the hard truth. And you need to treat others the same way. To have those relationships, you've got to be willing to hear as well as to talk.

But being a friend is not just about sharing the cold, hard truth. There are few things more rewarding than acting as a supporter and motivator for someone who you care about. Most times, friendship is all about fun. But it can also be emotional, meaningful, and even challenging. Like having a good friend, being a good friend makes you a better person. It increases your compassion, thoughtfulness, and kindness. With that said, don't just search for good friends, become one.

As you journey through life, sincerely think about your acquaintances, friends, and family. Consider your inner circle, and determine if the people closest to you are serving you in a positive way. Also look closer at those people you encounter on a day-to-day basis but couldn't tell me their last name even if I asked. They can also impact your success. Life is a game of inches, and those inches can be found in your acquaintances. Finally, work hard to get the most and give the most to your family. They are your greatest cheerleaders and will remain by your side through thick and thin. Do the same for them, and always cherish the time you have together.

Careers are difficult to build, but no one does it alone. A fantastic career is the culmination of all those people you have met along the way. Celebrate your success with your family and friends, and always remember that positive supporters can lead to a successful career.

CHAPTER 9

Career Builder #3

PROFESSIONAL COUNSELING:
DON'T KNOCK IT 'TIL YOU TRY IT

> "If you can, help others; if you cannot do
> that, at least do not harm them."
>
> —*Dalai Lama*

We have discussed the enormous value and power in surrounding yourself with people who can be true difference makers. Look around you. Are you hanging with strong mentors? Are you allowing your family and friends to support your growth? If so, you are moving in the right direction and building a successful career. But there are times when mentors, friends, and family are just simply not enough. There's a reason for professional counselors, just like there's a reason for auto mechanics. You can't always fix everything yourself. When you need help, seek a professional to determine the underlying cause of your personal or professional issues, and then implement a plan to help you through them.

Counseling offers three immediate benefits:

First, you get a fresh perspective on your life and the changes
you should make to rectify problems.

Second, if you need help in another area of your life, you already
understand the benefits of the process.

Third, your current counselor can help you find someone to
assist you in those other areas. If your faith is important to
you, consider a faith-based counselor. Don't be afraid to meet
with a couple of counselors to find the best one to coach you.

Many of us may feel that turning to professional help is tantamount to failure. It is the "If I cannot fix it myself, then I don't want to fix it at all" attitude. Still others may feel like they don't have an issue in the first place, yet find themselves spiraling out of control with no explanation as to "why." Even worse, there is an ongoing attitude problem many men may have: We often feel like admitting we have a problem or seeking professional help is a sign of weakness. But in truth, it takes strength and fortitude to acknowledge an issue and seek professional help for it.

Dr. Tim Irwin, *New York Times* bestselling author of *Impact*, shared with me this: "I believe counseling is of great value to people who are going through the stress that typically accompanies very demanding jobs. In my most recent book, *Impact*, I have three chapters on the importance of self-awareness, a major benefit of counseling. Many successful executives take advantage of coaches and mentors to that end. It also helps them navigate the often-challenging complexities of politics and power in the modern organization."

Counseling is a great thing. I learned this firsthand after my dad passed away in 2004. He had been on dialysis and suffering from extensive medical issues. A few days after he came home from the hospital, he slipped into a coma and died. The next month, while my wife, Angie, was pregnant with our second child, a hurricane hit our house. We had to abruptly move out. Then, two weeks after my second daughter was born, she suffered an acute life-threatening event and almost died. We had to rush her to the hospital.

Real stress is putting your two-week-old baby in an ambulance and riding to the hospital with an emergency medical team. She's doing great now, but, Lord have mercy, it was a rough time. Additionally, I'd severely injured my back and was experiencing chronic pain. These pain issues piled up on top of the other traumatic events in my life, and suddenly, I felt as if we were going through hell. I overcame the challenge but not without tremendous pain and suffering. Each morning, I started my day angry as sin. As the day progressed, so did my anger. My wife recognized I needed help, and she told me so.

She said, "You should go seek professional counseling."

My response (in typical male fashion), "No thank you. I have no interest in that."

She continued, "You need it because you're angry all of the time."

I defended myself. "Well, my kid almost died, my dad died, our house got messed up, and my back hurts all the time. It makes perfect sense that I am angry."

She said, "Well, you need to work it out."

As usual, Angie was right. So eventually, I started visiting with a therapist. But even then, I was embarrassed about it. To hide my appointments from staff members who had access to my calendar, I'd write on it "in a meeting." Despite my initial reluctance to acknowledge I needed help, the time I invested in therapy produced some of the best business counsel I'd ever received. I made extraordinary business decisions as I worked through the pain of my dad's death. The counseling enabled me to sort through my losses, clearly see my responses to them, and learn healthy ways to react to challenges I faced. Counseling provides immense help in clarifying your life.

LIKE SEEING A DOCTOR

Over time, you'll have health issues. You might find yourself with high blood pressure, an injured limb, appendicitis, or something else. What do you do? You go to a doctor and get help. Say you have a toothache. You wouldn't treat it yourself. You would call your local dentist and schedule an appointment. There would be an assessment, diagnosis, and treatment. That would be logical and even normal. I highly doubt you'd simply ignore the issue until it became completely unbearable and overwhelming. You likely know an unresolved toothache has the potential to turn into something much more significant. That is just one example of the physical ailment you could face.

But when it comes to life, not only physical issues can plague your progress—death, sadness, and other difficult things can impede it too. Treat each of these like a bad toothache or other physical ailment and go get help. Apply the same logic if you had twisted your ankle playing basketball or tweaked your back lifting a heavy couch.

One Thanksgiving weekend, a dear friend and coworker said, "Hey, John, can I come see you at home? I need to talk to you about three things."

I responded, "Okay."

"There's this deal, and this deal, and my wife's having an affair, so if we could talk about those three things it would be really helpful to me."

After a pause, I said, "Tell me the third one again." He did. We talked, and I said to him, "These challenges are like an awful car accident. If you were in a bad accident, we'd take you to the hospital. They'd treat your injuries, send you to physical therapy, and you'd understand it would take a long time to properly heal. But if you didn't get proper treatment, the wound could possibly flare up years later, creating more problems than you had at the beginning. Consider that. How much more painful would your recovery be? You might even get an infection or have to deal with a more serious condition."

After our talk, my friend decided to seek out counseling. He'd had a load of stress, but the counseling ultimately saved him.

That example I gave my friend about the positive effects of counseling illustrates the truth regarding the pain and suffering we often experience with regular emotional blows. You must work to heal those wounds in a healthy way. Sometimes the greatest injuries are the ones unseen. It is a lot easier to allow those to go untreated because they are less apparent to the outside world. Or so you think. Pain, anger, sadness, and grief are often the most obvious injuries because they go untouched. The cost of postponing attending to them is too high not to get appropriate treatment. As for my friend, he is now remarried and has a newborn. I am confident counseling helped him overcome his challenges and move in a positive direction.

A MANLY, MATURE DECISION

My friend is doing great now because he began taking care of his damage early. If you're thinking about getting married, get premarital counseling. If you get married and have an issue, see a counselor. One of the most masculine, courageous things a husband can do is say to his wife, "Let's go get help." Think of the potential consequences if you don't seek help when experiencing marital problems. The worst outcome would be divorce. But at the bare minimum, your happiness, effectiveness, and personal and professional lives could be impacted.

Counseling is a powerful, positive choice, and many highly respected professionals are choosing it. It is now more acceptable than ever, and CEOs, executives, and business leaders are often finding the time to speak with a professional. They might not even have a glaring and present issue. They may seek therapy simply because it helps keep them balanced.

I've heard story after story of professional athletes seeking sports therapists or psychologists. I could name at least a few PGA golfers who regularly attend sessions with a sports psychologist to help with their ability to visualize, reduce stress, and manage their anxiety. This treatment helps them produce and operate at a high level within their chosen profession. The same should be true with you.

CHOOSING THE RIGHT PROFESSIONAL

Just like a doctor or lawyer, find a counselor who specializes in your ailment. If you are having marital problems, seek a professional focusing in couples' therapy. If you find yourself fighting issues with drugs and alcohol, then a counselor focusing on addiction would likely be the right fit. If you are dealing with anxiety, depression, or obsessive behavior, find a specialist who focuses on mood disorders. There are literally specialists for every situation, personal issue, and overall concern.

Many people will tell you that they have avoided counseling because they just don't know where to look. Here are a few tips to help you find the right therapist or counselor for you:

Start with your friends and family. You may not be as open to the idea at first, but you'd be surprised at just how many of your friends and family rely on the assistance of a professional. If you feel comfortable sharing your personal issue with those who care the most about you, then turn to them for a referral. Just like you lean on friends for a referral to a mechanic or a roofer, the same can be true for a therapist.

Consider the right fit for you. As far as therapists go, consider those qualities that are important to you. Do you want someone who is straightforward or laid back? Would you prefer a male or female therapist? Do you want someone close to your home or someone in a more discreet location? Would you prefer a younger or older counselor? These may seem like trivial concerns, but you need to feel comfortable to relate to your trusted professional.

Check their credentials. It is just not about fit, but also experience. Use the vast amount of resources available to you on the Internet. Check rating sites, review professional achievements and awards, and confirm that your potential therapist or counselor has no pending or previous disciplinary issues. If you are going to invest time and money into a counselor, ensure that the person is well trained and experienced.

Come with an open mind. Walk into these appointments with an open mind. It is great that you decided to meet with a therapist, but you should also make the most of your time together. It may not always feel comfortable, but do your best to listen and be up front and honest. Your counselor will be able to help you the most if you are completely transparent.

Include your loved ones. Don't hide your meetings from your loved ones. Your friends and family are there to help you.

Offer them insight and feedback as to the things you are taking away from therapy. Consider asking your counselor if it makes sense to include a wife or husband or mother or father in a couple of sessions. That may help you get an outside perspective you couldn't see on your own.

Implement what you learn. Finally, implement what you learn from your counselor. Don't just show up to listen or talk. Remain introspective, and take their advice. It is amazing what the sound advice from a trained professional can do for you and your life. Spending time doing nothing but talking will only offer you marginal advances. But if you optimize the process by implementing the lessons learned, you will greatly increase the possibility of success.

Regaining emotional stability and strength is as valuable as the time, effort, and money you invest in your education. It not only benefits your career, but it also enhances your entire life. To ensure they are steadily progressing and hitting their targeted goals, the most successful people in the world constantly seek mentors, peers, and professionals to help them throughout their professional and personal lives.

To build a successful career, you must assemble an army around you to work as team members, cheerleaders, and pillars. With this group by your side, you will be well-positioned to continue in your extensive growth and personal development.

CHAPTER 10

Career Builder #4

BECOMING COACHABLE: WE ARE ALL TEACHABLE

"Each person holds so much power within themselves that needs to be let out. Sometimes they just need a little nudge, a little direction, a little support, a little coaching, and the greatest things can happen."

—*Pete Carroll*

In the previous chapters, we discussed the magnitude of finding strong mentors and building a support system that will help you achieve your goals. But after you meet these requirements, you will still have an enormous responsibility to find the right dream team for you and your career. And you have to be coachable. Most hiring employers will tell you that they often look for team members who are willing to listen and implement the lessons they are taught. Demonstrating you are coachable will not only help you obtain a great job, it will also help you develop. We often hear the term "coachable" in the context of sports. Head coaches always look to find talented young men and women who can be progressed and advanced. In fact, the greatest athletes of our time could all be deemed coachable in the context of their sports and positions.

The same is true in the professional realm. To build a successful career and make the most of your opportunities, you must learn and implement those lessons in order to improve and transform into a more valuable team member. This comes down to an endless desire to expand your knowledge by maintaining the right outlook, receptivity to feedback, and an unquenchable thirst to study and absorb your profession.

On-the-job coaching will benefit you the most if you maintain the right attitude toward it. Coachable people crave insight and instruction because they want to excel. Most young people would be successful if they did everything we told them to do in our office, but many times they simply choose not to, which is why they remain at a low or mediocre level. There are several reasons for this, but the recurring justifications for not being coachable generally include:

1. Excessive pride
2. Know-it-all attitude
3. Immaturity
4. Laziness
5. Lack of drive or motivation

Any one of these negative skills or traits can easily derail your career. But if you have more than one of them, you're probably not coachable. Employers covet coachable employees, and they will invest more time into people they perceive will learn from coaching and enjoy it the most. So the gains then become exponential.

Duke University basketball coach Mike Krzyzewski, known to most as Coach K, was asked in an interview, "How do you attract this great young talent? They play so well and graduate. How do you discover this talent and find these great players? What's your process?"

He explained that during recruiting interviews, he tells prospects, "You should say 'thank you' more often. The young men respond in one of two ways. Some say, 'Why, thank you, Coach K, for telling me that. I'll work on saying thank you more often. And thank you again.' Yet others say, 'What are you talking about—say thank you more often?'"

So why does he do that?

He shared, "Because when there are only three seconds left, and I say, 'I need you to pass it,' I expect them to say, 'Yes, sir,' and do it. And get it."

As Coach K illustrates, that is the true definition of coaching: trusting someone enough to simply listen and follow his or her lead. Now that doesn't mean you shouldn't think for yourself or form your own opinions. There is really no need for a yes man or woman. It simply means that there is a time for your opinion, and there is a time to listen and learn from those who are more experienced than you may be.

The fact that Coach K has led multiple Olympic basketball teams shows he knows what he's doing and exactly what he's talking about. His players will almost certainly be productive and succeed if they follow his lead and guidance. That is probably partly why, as of 2016, Duke had eighteen players in the NBA. That is the third most of all qualifying NCAA schools. Do your best to imitate these successful basketball players and listen to the successful people around you. Then work hard to put their advice into practice. Be quick to adjust based on their feedback, and then rise to the top of your career in the same way these coachable players did.

Being coachable is not just listening to your coaches and mentors, but it is also regularly demonstrating a specific type of skillset that can be trusted and respected. You must:

1. **Be accountable.** Coachable employees are ready to step up and take responsibility for their actions. Their bosses can count on them. When I started working, my goal wasn't to be the president of a company but to be the best employee. I wanted my bosses to know they could depend on me. When company leaders know you'll get the job done, regardless of the task, you become an important person to have around. Your career will grow, and you'll recognize more and more success.

2. **Learn from correction.** Coaching is the opposite of pride. It's the attitude of learning from correction. Great performers

want to be coached. They're open about their weaknesses and discuss them with an expert to reduce the blind spots they often face. They seek out constructive criticism to improve and as a result, they grow stronger and more effective. On the other hand, pride is weakness. Proud people refuse to acknowledge their faults, so they believe a lie. Pride prevents coaching, blocks growth, and ultimately leads to failure.

3. **Ask questions and show interest.** Coachable employees are engaged. They are focused on improving, and they show that interest by asking questions and listening to the answers provided. This demonstrates a genuine attention to the coaching they've received. Furthermore, it makes employers feel as if the employee is connected to improvement and thirsting for coaching.

I've seen so much talent wasted because employees refused to acknowledge their need to change. If you want to be successful, be someone who takes direction and does what is asked. You may not always understand why, but that's not your job. Sometimes you just have to invest some blind trust into the process. It might not always seem easy, but it can often lead to positive results. A willing response reinforces trust between employers and employees. If you trust whom you work for, you do what they ask. If you don't trust whom you work for, why are you working there in the first place?

A prime example of "coachability" is Tim Tebow. Most people know Tim as the Heisman and championship winning quarterback for the Florida Gators. He was then drafted into the NFL and had some great success during his limited time as a starter. As of the publication of this book, he is now making a run as a professional baseball player. He is an amazingly talented athlete, but that might not be his greatest attribute. Almost every coach he's played for has indicated he's humble and a genuinely coachable guy. When you see him, you like him because of his openness. In interviews, he doesn't talk about himself but about the team. As talented as he is, he looks for help to get better—an admirable, refreshing characteristic among young athletes. You'll hear from his coaches that they'd do anything for him, and they want him in the locker room and on the field.

Guys like Tebow are one in a million. But they shouldn't be. It isn't hard to be coachable. You just need to stay positive, listen, and implement changes to improve your development. There is no downside to this. It is all upside and potential gain. Dr. Samuel C. Certo, a professor of management at Rollins College, shared with me the following: "Uncoachables deprive themselves of the wisdom of others, while those that remain coachable benefit from that same wisdom."

Coaching pushes people to clearly view themselves. The mirror of introspection often reveals insecurities that can create even bigger problems if left unchanged. Some affect work, some don't. Either way, facing them enables you to deal with core issues that come into the open. For example, consider your family of origin, your dynamics about where you come from, and the events and people that shaped you. Seeing these more accurately and objectively can lead to a healthier, peaceful outlook, which not only benefits your personal life but also will spill over into your professional life.

Coaching can also offer you insight into your closest relationships and help you gain a better understanding of how they impact your overall productivity and evolution. For example, while I started counseling to deal with my father's death and some other health issues, the unexpected gain has been the positive influence it has had on me professionally. I've become more sensitive to how I come across to my employees and colleagues. I've recognized and dealt with specific triggers, and I determined some deeper wounds that needed bandaging. Acknowledging each of these helped me more positively interact with other people, at work and at home. I hadn't thought of myself as being coachable, but I listened to the feedback and I implemented changes.

There are many opportunities for coaching. Performance reviews are a great occasion for employers to set up coaching for their team, beginning with identifying and sharing strategic goals. It can be as simple as accomplishing a specific task or just understanding the bigger picture direction. Often it goes deeper to answer important questions: What motivates an employee to do certain things? What blocks the same person from doing other things? For instance, employees may say, "I want to be successful," but then when instructed to do certain things to be successful, they balk.

A salesperson may say, "I want to generate more sales." Then when the sales manager recommends networking, the employee resists and shies away from it. This leads to questions: "Why isn't he networking? Why wouldn't he want to do something that is critical to success?" The answer may be a deep insecurity about rejection, and part of the solution may be additional sales training.

At other times, learning a skill can rectify an apparent, immovable block. So often in business, I've found gaining proficiency in work skills reduces fear and eliminates intimidation. That will almost certainly help with personal development and offer monumental gains.

So from an employee perspective, you should remain open, maintain the right attitude, and search for coaching opportunities. Once you find them, take full advantage of them. Don't hesitate to offer feedback to your coaches and show them you are there for all the right reasons.

From an employer perspective, you have a responsibility to constantly offer your employees the occasion to be coached. Keep your eyes open to determine those employees who really want the coaching, then hone in on them and give them the resources they desire. You will see an exponential return on your time. If you find yourself struggling to implement a coaching environment around one or two employees, then ask yourself the tough questions and determine if they are even the right fit for your organization. If they are not interested in the resources you offer, then they really aren't interested in developing as an employee in the first place.

Great coaching builds great careers. As an employee, your success will be directly tied to your willingness to be a coachable student. You'll build better relationships with your superiors, and your leadership will be more willing to invest more time and money into your training. It is win-win, and remaining coachable is a huge career builder.

CHAPTER 11

Career Builder #5

CONNECTIONS: WHO DO YOU KNOW?

> "We cannot live only for ourselves. A thousand
> fibers connect us with our fellow men; and among
> those fibers, as sympathetic threads, our actions run
> as causes, and they come back to us as effects."
>
> —*Herman Melville*

Think about every person you've met over the course of your professional and personal life. My bet is you've found these connections have helped you navigate life and achieve greater success. I cannot begin to tell you the remarkable amount of assistance I have received from my connections. It is immeasurable. When it comes to your career, connections really matter. For every job obtained through classified ads, Internet job postings, social media blasts, or headhunters, I could point to ten more examples of professionals who secured a great job through the people they know. When it comes down to it, one of the main factors in getting a job is who you know, not how many different applications you submit. For many businesses, people skills and personal connections are the mortar between the building blocks of success.

As employees, we want to work with people we know and respect. This is a much more comfortable situation and likely a great indicator for future success. As a leader or hiring partner, we want to work with people who we know and trust. There is a certain level of ease when we already know the character of the person with whom we are working. That just goes to show that companies are predisposed to hire people with whom they are already connected. It is much easier and safer than going at it cold and determining if an unknown candidate is the right fit.

When my dad was young, he was a salesman. He liked to say, "The difference between good salespeople and great salespeople is that the great salespeople's stories are true." Connections make the world go 'round, so it should come as no surprise just how important your connections and relationships are or will be to your overall career success. Start building great connections through truthful relationships and stories. Incrementally, they will get you closer to the finish line. Rome wasn't built in a day, and neither will your connections be. So start by realizing that it takes time to build a strong network, and then get to work doing so one connection at a time.

NETWORK, NETWORK, NETWORK

Networking is the key to connecting with other people. Great salespeople and great networkers connect to others in a natural way. It is not forced, and this is among their strongest qualities. It carries a certain level of authenticity and genuineness, and most important, it takes time. To build a strong connection, you must do so one conversation and one interaction at a time. A strong networking opportunity may start with a cup of coffee and eventually turn into a lunch, dinner, or extracurricular activity like a golf outing.

One of the best ways to network with someone is to find commonalities. It would be easy to connect with your first boss from Boston if you were from there as well. This would be perceived as instant common ground. So when you're getting into business, develop networking relationships based on common interests and backgrounds.

For instance, people used to say that if you wanted to get into real estate, you had to drink and play golf. But I don't drink and I don't play golf. People recommended these activities because they provided a topic for conversation. If someone said, "Let's have a beer," then they could talk about the beer. If they played golf, then they could talk about golf. Sure, these are common hobbies of many real estate professionals, but the avenues for commonalities are endless. You don't need beer and golf, but you do need to learn to identify points of interest with other people.

For example, let's say you live in Florida and attended Florida State University, the University of South Florida, the University of Central Florida, Miami University, or one of the other great schools in the state. That would make you part of a large and influential alumni base. There's an excellent chance that if you went up to someone in your state and referenced your alma mater, they'd smile and start trading war stories with you. And you'd start to connect with that person extraordinarily fast. You can then dive even deeper and find out if that person is a member of a fraternity or sorority you belong to. I bet the two of you share a favorite restaurant or enjoy discussing a specific Florida college sports team.

My point: It is not hard to connect with people. There are hundreds of networking opportunities and commonalities. You might not have the same upbringing or background as someone else, but you can find some common area to connect.

The business world works through networking, relationships, and connecting. Build on your strengths, the things that you're passionate about. Understand where you're called to be and get to know others with similar interests outside of the subject of your degree. Explore new hobbies and associations such as sailing or tennis and meet new people.

Make those connections.

CONNECTIONS ARE EVERYWHERE

Because my dad was a pastor and a civil rights leader, matters of faith and civil rights have always been important to our family. When I got into collegiate education, I discovered that of the one hundred six historically black colleges in the country, none had real estate programs.

That was disturbing because black colleges were created to deal with issues in the black community. Real estate should have been a logical part of the curriculum because it would open more opportunities for financial stability and success. But it was missing. That was a glaring issue to me, since property owners tend to be more connected to their communities and have greater satisfaction living there.

In the past, slavery and Jim Crow laws prevented a segment of our population from owning real estate. The Civil Rights Movement opened doors, but the skills needed to help you go through them remained absent. A void in the education system hindered families from pursuing success in real estate. When you connect the dots, you discover a direct line to an issue like Ferguson.

So I decided to do something about that. I asked one of our interns to start a real estate club at his school, Florida A&M University (FAMU). We then persuaded the school to have its first real estate class. The former intern and I stayed in touch, and I emailed him a couple of summers ago. He shared with me that the White House had an initiative to make some important changes in historically black colleges. I wanted him to get me a phone call with the decision makers on Capitol Hill. He wasn't sure he could make that connection but agreed to follow my lead when I told him to "just make an attempt at it."

When he got back to me, he said, "They want to have a call with us." We had that call while I was driving the family van back from vacation. I kept the kids quiet because I was on the phone with the White House and this college student who had set up the call. I said to the number two person overseeing the White House's historically black colleges' and universities' (HBCUs) initiative, "I believe this is a gap in the Civil Rights Movement." I was unsure how he would respond, but he said, "I think you're right."

Then we got lucky. About a month later, Thomas, the intern, was graduating with his MBA from FAMU. Guess who was the keynote speaker? The number one national executive for the HBCU. We secured a meeting with him. I sent Thomas by himself. He crushed it. Then we had a few more meetings. In October 2016, I spoke twice at the Congressional Black Caucus in Washington, DC. I also met President Barack Obama, Martin Luther King III, and Congressman John Lewis.

Remember MLK's "I Have a Dream" speech? On that day he made that address, he was one of six speakers. Only one of those speakers is still alive—Congressman Lewis.

Think about that. I went from a casual conversation and simple idea to meeting the President of the United States. How did that happen? We tried. We asked. We took a swing. And we connected every single time. As much as I'd love to credit this success to my efforts, it really just came down to the power of networking. And at the end of it all, they gave me an Underground Railway award from the US Senate.

On that day, I sat on stage with Ernie Hudson, the actor who played Winston in *Ghostbusters*. He sat to my left. A United States congresswoman sat on my right. The topic for the day's speeches was "150 Years a Slave." I was told nothing about what I was to speak on. But then the congresswoman leaned toward me and said, "One speaker is talking about the past. Another is discussing the present. I want you to talk about the future."

I said, "You got it." And I wrote my speech sitting next to Winston from *Ghostbusters*.

This story is a wonderful example of how meaningful connections really live within purposeful endeavors. For connections and networking to truly matter, you must connect with people through your heart and soul. It must have meaning and occur at an emotional level. As I mentioned a few pages before, my father distinguished great salespeople from good salespeople by the sincerity of their words—"the great salespeople's stories are true." Truth matters because it helps you connect through authenticity. My challenge to you: Go further and reach out to make real connections with people with whom you share common qualities. Work on your skills to find people who share your beliefs and morals and have a character similar to your own. Fighting for equality remains an extremely important responsibility to me. I have learned a lot from interacting with people from different backgrounds and life experiences. But the greatest lesson is that connections occur through the genuine desire to create meaningful change.

This attitude really extends beyond that example, as it is applicable to important moments in life. Think about the connections that occur during times of need. Ever attend a funeral? Visit a friend or family member in the hospital? Spend hours on the phone with a friend going through a tough time? Those are the moments when emotional connections occur. They are stronger than others and have substantial meaning. They stay with people and are not easy bonds to break.

So as you build your network, target emotional bonds too. They aren't formed overnight, and they take more effort and more energy than the arm's-length friendships you might have. But connections built purely on heart and soul are often the most rewarding types. They stay with you, transcend time, and leave the most lasting impressions.

BUILDING A NETWORK

Let's highlight the best ways to create connections and build a strong network:

Get Involved. One of the most successful ways to build a strong career and network is by getting involved. Look for organizations, endeavors, and strategic partnerships that will help you along the way. For example, wherever you move after graduation, get involved with alumni from your school. If you end up somewhere with no boosters or other alumni association, start one. You can be president. This sets up commonality and gives you a place to start. As you build your career, you'll discover other ways to get to know people.

Help Others. I have found that, over the course of my own career, the best way to create connections is by helping people in need. Joining a philanthropic or charitable organization positions you with other generous souls, and you can likely spend your time together learning more about one another. As you build these relationships, you'll find your new friends and colleagues are willing to extend themselves and help you along the way.

Be Social. No matter what city you live in, there are tons of opportunities to connect with likeminded people. More and more organizations are popping up around town and offering mass networking events. Each of these offers a bountiful arena to connect with new people who share the same interests and age group as you. You never know when one of these people will be hiring or looking for their company. Take the chance and put yourself out there, as you never know what can come from it.

Social Media. With the advent of various social media outlets, networking is easier than ever. Start by ensuring you have updated your information across outlets like Facebook, LinkedIn, Instagram, and any other channels you regularly use. Connect with people who share regular interests with you. If you are on LinkedIn, go ahead and endorse them. Write a nice referral on their Facebook page. Show them you care and build a strong connection with each of them.

Keep in Touch. One of the biggest mistakes people often make is losing touch with their great connections. You took the time to build a network, so remain in contact with it. It doesn't take much. Send a connection an article of interest you previously read, invite them to coffee, or just drop them a handwritten note every so often. Staying in the front of their minds is a meaningful way to remain in contact and build your network.

Always Be on the Lookout. I always tell people that you never know where your next connection is coming from, so always carry a few business cards and make sure to give them out. Networks are built one connection at a time. The more people with whom you interact, the better you'll be in the long run.

Utilize Your Friends and Colleagues. Your friends and coworkers are some of the best avenues to network and build connections with. I regularly use my current network to expand to other people. Ask your friends or coworkers for a few strong connections. Request that they make direct introductions, and then follow up with lunch or coffee. Taking this one step further, check out your friends' connections on sites like LinkedIn to determine if there is a strategic connection you'd like to make. There is no shame in targeting people you can help and people who can help you.

Alan Collins, Author of *Unwritten HR Rules: 21 Secrets for Attaining Awesome Career Success in Human Resources*, said, "Pulling a good network together takes effort, sincerity, and time." But to build a successful career, potentially there is nothing more powerful than those people with whom you connect. Start building your network as early as college, and work hard to stay in touch with these people. They will come to form the foundation of support and structure for you in the forthcoming years. Once you build a strong network, remain connected with it. It takes just a little bit of time to maintain a positive energy between you and your network. A man's or woman's success can be measured by those people with whom they are connected. If you feel the same way, take every single opportunity to build a network that you can serve and that serves you well.

PART IV

Creating a Unified Life

Are you excited to build a remarkably successful career? If you've come this far in this book, you have learned about many of the tools that will get you on your way. We have discussed career killers and career builders. Our career killers consist of:

Career Killer #1: Drugs and Alcohol: No One Likes the Life of the Party After the Party

Career Killer #2: Sex: Monogamy Is Magnificent

Career Killer #3: Greed: Money *Can* Be the Root of All Kinds of Evil

Career Killer #4: Temperament: No One Likes a Hothead

Career Killer #5: Pride: Humility Always Wins Out

After considering and then hopefully avoiding each of these, we can shift our attention to building a fantastic career, which consists of:

Career Builder #1: Mentors: It Takes a Village to Succeed

Career Builder #2: Relationships: Family and Friends Lead the Charge

Career Builder #3: Professional Counseling: Don't Knock It 'Til You Try It

Career Builder #4: Becoming Coachable: We Are All Teachable

Career Builder #5: Connections: Who Do You Know?

Work to make each of these important considerations a part of your life. They are integral pillars that will support you as you grow, develop, and evolve personally and professionally. But your work is not done. You need to take just one more step: Connect your personal life to your professional one. Harmony between the two is truly the path to happiness. You do this by:

1. Developing passion for your life
2. Building a strong personal and professional brand
3. Choosing the right city for you

Let's unpack each one at length.

CHAPTER 12

Passion: Personal Happiness Grows into Professional Success

"There is no passion to be found playing small—in settling for a life that is less than the one you are capable of living."

—*Nelson Mandela*

It didn't happen overnight, but I absolutely love what I do for a living. So much so that it doesn't even feel like work. I awake each day, roll out of bed, and hit the ground running in eager anticipation of the work that lies ahead. I am one of those lucky few who is extraordinarily passionate about my chosen career. Some of the most successful people in the world will tell you that their success derives in large part from their passion for their work.

Think about your day-to-day activities. Wouldn't you agree that you enjoy those activities that you are most passionate about? Maybe it is your family or friends, following a sports team, or even a hobby like golf. My bet is you not only look forward to that time but also feel like it passes with the snap of a finger. Nothing else seems to matter, and the world just seems right. Your heart, mind, body, and soul are all fully engaged in those moments. That is true passion. Now, there are times you might still find trouble getting out of bed and starting your day. It happens to the best of us. But for the most part, our collective goal is to feel passionate and purposeful about what we do every day.

To build a successful career, you must choose an area or profession that you are remarkably passionate about. Let's look at some of the most successful people in their respective industries and their opinions on passion. To name a few:

Edgar Allen Poe said, "With me poetry has not been a purpose, but a passion."

Maya Angelou said, "My mission in life is not merely to survive, but to thrive; and to do so with some passion, some compassion, some humor, and some style."

Oprah Winfrey said, "Passion is energy. Feel the power that comes from focusing on what excites you."

Jon Bon Jovi said, "Nothing is as important as passion. No matter what you want to do with your life, be passionate."

Albert Einstein said, "I have no special talents. I am only passionately curious."

Think about each of these successful individuals. Consider how much they accomplished during their professional lives. Some of them literally changed the way we understand the world, and they all had at least one trait in common: passion. So if it is good enough for the likes of Poe, Angelou, Winfrey, Bon Jovi, and Einstein, shouldn't you work to find something you are passionate about?

DON'T SKIMP ON PASSION

Too many people wake up one day and realize they are unhappy, unfulfilled, and literally dread going to work every day. I don't blame them for those feelings. But take that group and consider how many of those same people repeat this practice day after day after day. They recognize just how unhappy they are in their current position and then remain there for most of their professional lives. Don't skimp on passion. Successful people build passionate careers and are extremely willing to make a change when they lose that passion or simply cannot locate it. Think about all the famous people who made a change midstream to find their true calling.

Most people don't know Julia Child worked in advertising and media before she wrote her first cookbook at the age of fifty, eventually becoming one of the most famous French cuisine chefs in the world.

Before Michael Bloomberg became mayor of New York City, he was the CEO of a financial software, data, and media company.

How about the designer Vera Wang? She was a figure skater and journalist before starting in fashion at the age of forty.

Before Dwayne "The Rock" Johnson joined the World Wrestling Federation and became one of the most famous actors of our time, he was a football player and played linebacker for the Miami Hurricanes.

And finally, Ronald Reagan, the fortieth president of the United States, was a film actor first.

Each of these respectable men and women followed their passion and in doing so found wild success. There really is no better and surefire way to excel at what you do than if it is fueled by driven passion. For every successful career out there, passion is one of the most important drivers for that individual. So with that said, what are some of the steps you can take to develop a strong passion for your career?

BUILDING A PASSIONATE LIFE

1. Invest Time and Energy. First, start today by making a commitment to set aside one hour a week to totally focus on building a passionate career. Write it on your calendar. Lock it in like going to class or scheduling an important meeting. If you're at a significant juncture, whether graduation or in your career, consider making that an hour a day. How do you do that? Drop some things. Watch less television. Reduce video time.

Focus on advancing your career. Invest your time, energy, and resources for the next six months to obtain significant results.

During this hour, assess where you are in your career. Ask yourself questions like:

Am I satisfied in the present structure of my profession?
Am I progressing at a rate with which I am comfortable?
Am I truly happy at work?

The answers to each of these questions will help you capture a 20,000-foot view of where you stand in your professional life. If you are unsatisfied with your answers, then it is clearly time to consider a change or at least a shift in your responsibilities.

2. Identify Your Passion. Second, consider what passion means, where it comes from, and how to get it. What do you do when you're encouraged to follow your passion? Identifying your passion isn't always easy. But start by making a list of those things that really provide you with pure and unfiltered joy. For example, let's say that animals are high on your list. If so, then consider professions that keep you close to animals. Perhaps you are destined to work at a veterinarian's office, or a specialty animal store, or even to volunteer at The Humane Society. Once you make your list, review it often. It might change from time to time, but it will help you identify what you truly love and use that as a jumping off point to determine the best career fit for you.

When you find and chase your passion, you have to develop some technical skills. For instance, I love marketing. I'm attracted to it. Although I don't have professional training in it, I do it all the time in my business. Sometimes I think I should have majored in marketing in college. To develop this passion, I read books, listen to podcasts, and research marketing on the Web. I even work closely with our marketing department to really learn how they do their job. This is just one area in which I am passionate, and I take all the time I can to soak in the subject matter and work on marketing. It is not enough to love something. You also must work hard to develop a skill-set that propels your progress in your passion so that you can reach a level of success with it and continue to pursue it.

A few years before my dad had kidney failure, I didn't know anything about dialysis; but once he went on it, I learned all about it. Twenty-five percent of dialysis patients die every year. In addition, it is like a part-time job. Before my dad passed away, he spoke to doctors at several dialysis conventions teaching them how to deal with the grieving process. Our family had been unfamiliar with it before this, but we learned about it and got involved. This became our passion, and it helped us deal with an otherwise difficult situation. Passion helped heal our troubles.

3. Be Passionate About Who You Are. Some people have trouble locating things that they are passionate about. That may end up being an internal problem, not an external one. You need to know yourself well and recognize how you tick. I used to think people either were passionate or weren't, but I've come to realize that you can choose passion. Think about the role you play as a student. Students often ask me whether they should continue their education and go to graduate school. Whenever a student asks if he should get his MBA, I ask, "Why do you want to get it?"

"I don't want to limit my future by not having my MBA."

This answer isn't good. Here's my comeback to it: "People who don't know what they want to do with their lives won't know what they want simply by getting an MBA."

Getting an MBA or any other advanced degree should be a focused decision. For instance, if you have an undergraduate degree in retail or architecture and you decide you want to be the president of the company someday, then go back and get an MBA. Or you have a political science degree and decide that you want to go into real estate, get a master's degree in real estate.

Many people take routes to acquire things they believe they are passionate about, but then realize they never cared about those things. Imagine how you'd feel if you spent the money and invested the time in an MBA, only to realize you never even needed it or wanted it. It happens all the time with law school grads and med school grads. They follow a "passion," only to realize it was never *their* passion.

This is just one example of the importance of knowing yourself inside and out. First, you must be passionate about who you are so you can figure out what makes you happy externally. Internal first, external second: That is how you don't misplace your passion for something you never really wanted in the first place.

CHANGE YOUR SCENARIO

Passion changes your position in life. It opens doors, unlocks potential, and gives you the endless fuel to excel in your career. It builds success at a remarkable level. But you must change your scenario and invite passion in. Once you locate it and are clear about what motivates you, there is no stopping your professional success. Often, change is scary, but it can be the most direct path to improve yourself and your situation. Change the whole scenario. Have a great attitude and smile no matter what's going on.

Far too often, I see unhappy employees continue to stink it up at work, unaware just how obvious their lack of passion is to those around them. They do their job, but it is apparent that they are miserable. Only you can change your scenario.

What would happen to a fantastic employee like this? He or she would get promoted or hired by someone else immediately. A poor attitude blocks people at every level from higher achievement because they think, "I'm not passionate about anything, especially this!" They mistakenly think passion and the right path will just appear. They won't.

You've got to choose passion and go after things hard. The more you do, the more your life will be enriched. Opportunities will open. Better yet, you'll enjoy your life and your relationships more.

My life now is wonderful. I wake up and feel like each day is an amazing canvas to paint. It's the result of years of doing things I really didn't want to do—things that were the building blocks for what I get to do now. In addition, I now have more choices in my life.

Take your passion to make an impact. We've all heard the life philosophy "it's not all about you"—and it's true. In finding ways to let your passion, energy, and creativity help others, you'll reap benefits, often intangible but nevertheless real. Wherever you end up, you can take your passion within your career and make an impact too. Most people don't ever take the chance.

CHAPTER 13

Connecting Your Life: Building a Brand

"Branding demands commitment; commitment to continual re-invention; striking chords with people to stir their emotions; and commitment to imagination. It is easy to be cynical about such things, much harder to be successful."

—*Sir Richard Branson*

Successful professionals view their career as a specific brand with a very focused purpose. Most people go to work each day willing to fulfill a specific goal or laundry list. They don't view their career as a brand, they just believe they fulfill a role. But building a brand is a remarkably powerful way to create something bigger than yourself. Imagine that your brand is a small business, and your goal is to build that business as quickly as possible. What steps would you take to do that? What would you do every day to build a foundation for your brand? My hope is that this chapter will help you to accomplish two things:

1. Shift your paradigm from employee or worker to a brand
2. Take meaningful steps to build a marketable brand to project to the world

Marketing and salespeople know the value of establishing a positive brand or image connected with them or with a product or service they offer. This outreach extends far and wide when used properly and can effectively bring you to the awareness of many. So where do we begin? The most influential and important place to build your brand is through social media.

SOCIAL MEDIA IS . . . YOUR BRAND

Want to create a brand? Want to elevate your career? The only logical place to start is in the wide reach of the Internet. Now more than ever, consumers, employers, and business leaders search the Internet to obtain a glimpse into you and your brand. That then becomes a double-edged sword. On one hand, poor Internet presence can really hurt you. However, as you'll find in this chapter, a strong social media imprint can make the difference in your brand and your professional success.

So how do you create a strong social media brand? Start by considering all the mediums available to you. These include sites like Facebook, LinkedIn, Instagram, YouTube, Twitter, Pinterest, Google+, and many more. To start, remember that anything and everything you project to the world becomes part of your brand. That politically charged post. That picture of you doing a keg stand. That racially insensitive statement. Every one of these, good or bad, becomes your brand. So for starters, remember the golden rule of social media: *That which you project to the world becomes part of your brand.* No matter what social media outlets you use, always put your best foot forward. Be positive and encouraging. It's the best tactic for leveraging social media. Draw people to your brand so your followers will get better through your encouragement. Let that positive position be who you are.

CLEAN IT UP

Understand who's looking at your social media pages and why they are looking. Yours can be personal but should suggest professionalism. For example, my LinkedIn page has videos, podcasts, resources, and connections to groups. You can become market dominant through LinkedIn. However, while few people leverage that tool, you can and should. Regarding LinkedIn and other social media or marketing, use these common questions to plan your social media strategy to create a thoughtful brand:

- Who do you want to reach? Define your audience.
- What do you want to say? Consider your content.
- How do you want to say it? Edit and clarify it.
- When do you want to say it? Choose a regular time of day and frequency of posting.
- Where do you want to say it? Determine which media you'll use.

Answer these questions. Be disciplined and consistent. Take calculated risks. Above all, structure your content to be uplifting, while planning to encourage others. With that said, here are the five must-dos for social media branding:

1. Be positive. No one likes a naysayer.
2. Put your best foot forward. You only have one chance to make a first impression.
3. Help others. Social media is a great way to support other people.
4. Keep your sites updated. Your bio, your professional picture, and your work experience should all be current.
5. Remain active. Don't let your page go dormant. Regularly post thoughtful comments and relevant ideas.

Social media is the least expensive way to project a very specific message to the world about who you are—a message that you completely create and choose. So even if you are an employee for a large business, that is just one part of your brand. It is not your complete brand, just a piece of the puzzle. Your brand is so much more. It is your previous work experience, your accomplishments, your education, your endorsements, and your network. That is a better picture of your brand, and you can use social media to convey it. Your brand is simply where you start. Once you create it, you have to leverage it. What avenues can we take to leverage your brand to increase your viability for success?

LEVERAGING YOUR BRAND

Once you create your brand, you have a remarkable opportunity to use it to enhance your career. There are several ways to accomplish this. For starters, you can do a great job of leveraging your brand simply by using it to care for others. In the past, I have used my social media to connect with people. I like congratulating people, thanking people, and honoring people, because these things don't happen enough in our society. Because many people are beaten down, I look for ways to reverse discouragement. I like to emphasize the positive and find solutions, going against the tide of people who waste time complaining instead of taking action to fix problems. How many times have you logged onto your social media accounts only to notice colleague after colleague making negative and disparaging comments? It can really bum you out, right? My point is that you can use your brand to be an elevator, and a positive contributor to society. It may take more energy at the beginning to resolve issues and find positive things to discuss, but in the end, solutions energize everyone who get involved. The opposite is true of complainers. Whining takes less energy in the beginning, but that attitude always drains and de-energizes people in the end.

As you continue to use your social media profiles to do great things, you must leverage your social media sites through creating strong connections. I always kid that there are two types of social media users: The first type have a very small and well-conceived group of people with whom they connect. The second type will connect with everyone and have thousands of connections, few of whom they even know. I'd suggest you have something in between. You want many connections because they can unlock doors. You can use them to determine who they know and who you'd like to know in their networks. But you don't want to connect with people you barely even know. They may post questionable comments and articles that then appear on the feeds of your other connections. That's when problems can occur. So at a minimum, take the time to vet out any potential connection to determine if he or she can help you and if he or she is consistent with your morals and character.

Leveraging your social media is not just about connecting with people. Sites like LinkedIn and Facebook allow you to connect with companies as well. If you are looking for a job, follow some targeted companies on social media. Support them and post comments on their sites like, "You're doing a great job." Get out there and be aware. By doing this, you forge a connection with these companies. Make a list of the top ten companies and the top ten people you'd like to work for. Follow them through social media and learn about them. Use that information to prepare for your job interviews and then go with a fantastic list of questions because there's so much information available. Prepare to meet people you choose by becoming familiar with them. Access the material available. Analyze it. Apply it to your career path.

You can also do this for job reviews if you want to explore other opportunities in your company. In addition, to further equip you, subscribe to the YouTube channel for your targeted company and see what hot topics they are posting.

As you are connecting, you have a wonderful opportunity to use social media to create meaningful leverage. For example, at Crossman & Company, we use our social media reach to further our brand through our creation called *Guide to Commercial Real Estate*. Years ago, I was advising a global real estate trade organization and wanted to get them to create a guide, but the guy I talked to blocked my suggestion; he didn't want to work that hard. So using social media, I found out where the president of his organization went to undergraduate school, bought him a T-shirt, and redid our guide with his company's logo on the front. I overnighted it to him.

The president called me. "I love this. We should create this for our organization." And I thought, *I know you should.* They did in fact create a guide, and they used it for a long time. Tools like this are available in every profession. If yours doesn't have one, maybe you're the one to write it. If you Google real estate, sixty-four million hits come up and ours is number four. That all started years ago when we used social media to build a brand and leverage other opportunities.

In addition to meeting and connecting with a boatload of interesting people, social media lets you leverage your brand through strategic alliances and relationships. Whatever your career or your brand, become active in the appropriate organizations and put them on your resume. If you're still a student, it's impressive. It's the first thing I look for on student resumes. It matters more if you're out of school and working. Again, this holds true of other careers and their appropriate associations. Sadly, despite telling thousands of students this, I rarely see it. Thus, you can bet the easiest and most effective way to get involved is by subscribing to social media channels and regularly following them. They'll keep you updated about upcoming events and local opportunities to get involved.

But don't stop there. Social media offers you millions of occasions to get involved in membership associations. First, membership shows that you've invested in the industry. Second, it demonstrates that you're trying to learn. You'll get blast emails and magazines that help you learn the jargon and the players in the industry. They publicize events you can attend at a discount. Your membership will be inexpensive as a student, but skyrocket when you become a professional. Get in early.

Imagine this: You interview for a job that will pay for your membership and you say, "I've got that covered for now. I already have a student membership and remain involved in social media outlets." You'd be offering to save that company several hundred dollars. Think how impressive that would be.

If you've already graduated and have a membership, it shows commitment. And that was just one part of your brand.

Social media is one of the most cost effective ways to build a brand. But once you create that brand, you must leverage it. This section should help you connect and create a meaningful network that you can use to elevate your professional success. Remember: *Your brand gets you employed.* Don't believe me? I can give you hundreds of examples of young men and women who leverage social media to get a job. But the truth is that it was their brand on social media that really sealed the deal. More and more employers are looking to the Internet for job postings and hiring opportunities. They are also "interviewing" clients and doing background checks on social media sites to see what kind of person you really are. That is partially why you must be considerate of every last post you make.

SOCIAL MEDIA = YOUR BRAND
= CAREER SUCCESS

I probably sound like a broken record, but social media builds successful careers, but only if you look at it as an integral part of your brand. Forget the notion that you are just an employee, or just an executive, or just a team member. You are a small company with a distinct brand, and you should work to attract people to your brand. You do that by remaining positive, projecting a positive social media brand, strategically connecting with people and organizations, and being an active poster on social media.

There are so many opportunities available, and the best part is that most of them are either free or low cost. At minimum, create a LinkedIn and Facebook page. Connect with friends and professional colleagues you respect, then thank them for their connection, endorse their skills, and always congratulate them on a success. The truth is that the Internet is continuously growing into the most powerful networking opportunity around. So you have to create an airtight brand to project to the world via the World Wide Web.

Building a successful career goes hand in hand with the brand you build. Invest just a few minutes each day in remaining active and putting your best electronic foot forward.

CHAPTER 14

Building Community:
Location, Location, Location

"Every successful individual knows that his
or her achievement depends on a community
of persons working together."

—*Paul Ryan*

The final way to ensure you connect your personal life to your professional one to manifest happiness is by choosing the right city for you. Building a successful career often comes down to location, location, location. Far too often, grads choose a city to live in based on the nightlife, social setting, or even professional sports teams. However, one of the most important pieces of your professional puzzle comes in the form of exactly where you build your career.

During many of my job interviews, I often ask students where they'd prefer to live. The common response is, "Anywhere." Then I ask, "Have you been to Detroit?" Even though I'm kidding, I use that city to demonstrate that picking a location is an extremely important decision. I have heard story after story of graduates accepting jobs all over the world. They travel to their new hometown, excited at the possibilities and opportunity. Then they begin to miss their families, don't necessarily connect to the local community, and simply cannot create a familiar and comfortable life. They then have buyer's remorse and are extremely unhappy outside of their career. This begins to impact their day-to-day behaviors and attitude, and they eventually fizzle out, looking for any way to jump ship and find a new job.

In the end, it all comes down to location. And the smartest job seekers choose a career location based on three important variables:

1. Connection to the city
2. Opportunity in the city
3. Relationships in the city

We will unpack each of these as we move through this chapter. But before we do, always remember that "anywhere" is not the answer to the question "Where would you live and work?" Instead, I'd recommend that you say, "I'm flexible, but my number one pick is Charlotte. However, I know you have offices in Dallas and Chicago, and I believe those cities would be good fits as well." Name your preference and follow with a clear statement of flexibility. It won't limit you because there may be a position in the very place you want to work. Because remember: Accept "anywhere" and you might just get the middle of nowhere.

CONNECTION TO THE CITY

You *must* feel a connection to your career city. Think about moving to a city like going on a first date. Sure, you will certainly need to get to know the person you're sitting across the table from, but you likely have prequalified him or her. You've determined he or she is single, has basic similar interests, and can likely connect with you at least in a basic and fundamental manner. The same is true with choosing a city for your career. You don't have to know every intimate detail about your chosen city, but it has to generally be a good fit.

For example, if you just absolutely cannot stand cold weather, avoid cities like Chicago and Boston. You won't survive even one winter. Maybe you like to avoid the red-hot Southern summers. If so, my hometown of Orlando is likely the wrong location for you.

But weather is not the only deal breaker. If you like live music, pick a city with a budding live music scene. Foodie? Try Los Angeles or New York. Enjoy culture? Seattle and Portland. Maybe you enjoy the mountains and like an outdoor lifestyle? Colorado or Austin might be the way to go. The point is that much of your happiness and ability to remain engaged and succeed is often linked to the connection you have with your city.

Success is the result of many decisions. One of those decisions is ensuring your life outside of work is a positive and meaningful one. To that end, you must choose a part of the world where you are content and happy. Do a good job of understanding your personality and what makes you thrive. Then match those needs with a city that can fulfill them.

Review the following questions as you narrow down the environment you wish to explore:

- What activities outside of work make you happy?
- What are the life conditions that you prioritize?
- What type of environment did you grow up in?
- What do you thrive on?
- What type of person do you enjoy working and interacting with?

These are all important questions to answer to ensure that you are choosing a city that meets your personal needs so you can excel in your professional life.

OPPORTUNITY IN THE CITY

Here's the thing about life: If you pick something you're passionate about, you'll do fine with your income. If you want to be a fifth-grade math teacher and love it, you'll be excited every day about going to work. That's why you should pick something you care about that aligns with your personality. Talk to friends. Take a Myers-Briggs test. Connect the dots. For instance, an analytical person who gets a sales job will not only be terrible at it, but miserable.

My wife used to be an actress. Early in her career, she'd go to the mall, walk around, and do a little survey about herself by asking people, "Look at me. What do you think I look like?" It helped her decide which jobs to interview for by how people perceived her. Other actors have used the same approach.

When you think about a good-looking male lead like Christian Bale or Ryan Gosling, you know you probably won't see either of them playing a nerd. It's not that they don't have the acting skills, but it's not how they're perceived. Actors know that about themselves. It's the same with businesspeople.

But passion isn't enough. If those same actors and actresses hung around Houston, Texas, they might never have gotten their big break. They decided to move to Hollywood and roll the dice to reach their dreams. To that end, when making a career choice, you must consider the city in which you will reside. It is highly unlikely you'll make it big in Hollywood if you are hanging out in Hollywood, Florida. Let's say you want to be a trader, then New York and the Stock Exchange might just be the place for you. Different cities offer you different opportunities. Since location is everything, make sure you choose a city that is completely aligned with your overall goals and career path.

An easy way to determine the best cities for you is to visit websites like Forbes.com or related career-focused landing spots that categorize the best cities for particular career paths. You'll learn more about the best cities for techies, for real estate, for finance, for lawyers, for doctors, and for much more. Match your career path to the city that can best pave the way.

RELATIONSHIPS IN THE CITY

Finally, choose a city where you have relationships. I cannot tell you how many times I have seen friends and family members open doors for young professionals. When it comes to business, relationships really matter, perhaps more than anything else. Consider those relationships you simply cannot live without. Do you currently live close to your parents? Your brothers or sisters? Your best friends? Could you imagine life without them by your side?

If not, then don't choose a city far from them. Eventually, you will find yourself homesick, and you will likely feel torn between your current job and your desire to be closer to family and friends. New cities offer new opportunities and new friends. But you have to at least assess the possibility that you might not create any meaningful connections.

To varying degrees, we all need love and friendship. Our friends and family support us, expand our network, and offer meaningful opportunities to advance and progress in our careers. These friends and family members eventually become your biggest cheerleaders and even referral sources. I know lawyers and doctors who have built remarkable practices based solely on the friends and family members with whom they grew up. Recognize that starting fresh in a new city is exciting, but not nearly as easy as building a career in a city where you already have seeds planted.

If you do move to a new city and decide you want to organically expand your network, here is a list of ways you can:

- Make a list of everyone you know in the area and leverage it.
- Grow your friends and alumni network.
- Set mentorship goals and make a plan.
- Purchase business cards and hand them out.
- Stay in close touch with your professors.
- Become a good listener, always open to advice and guidance.
- Join professional organizations and attend conferences.
- Continue to network, network, network.

As discussed throughout this chapter, "anywhere" should never be the response to questions pertaining to your preferred job locations. The best careers are built at the right place at the right time. But you must be in the right place first. Be picky when considering where you want to live. Sure, it is natural to want to be close to home; however, many people will tell you the best decision they made was to follow their dreams and take a leap of faith. But always remember:

Don't make an emotional decision.
Don't simply follow your friends.
Don't accept a job in an unfamiliar city out of mere desperation.
Don't settle for something that doesn't fit your needs and lifestyle.
Don't be scared to move back home.

Successful careers mean different things to different people. Progressing, evolving, and making money are just part of what make great careers great. Consider all your options, think about how you'd enjoy moving to a city, and then make an informed decision based on opportunity, connection, and most importantly, location.

CHAPTER 15

Can You Have It All?
Happiness Is Within Reach

"Happiness is when what you think, what
you say, and what you do are in harmony."

—*Mahatma Gandhi*

Passion, brand, and location. At first glance they seem like unrelated concepts, but they each play a remarkably important role in your ability to secure a happy lifestyle. If you awake each day passionate about your job, connected to the world around you in a positive way, and supported by the community where you live, you will achieve synchronicity in your life. It doesn't just happen. It takes calculated choices and an internal desire to just be happy.

We've spent most of this book discussing how to build a successful career, but the truth is that we are just focused on helping you build a happy life. Your career is an extremely important part of your overall happiness, but this chapter will outline other considerations that may be just as important. At the end of the day, that is really all that matters. Happiness is subjective. Some view freedom as happiness, while others perceive financial wealth as happiness. Still others just want a big family, while some might want to travel the world. This is not a one-size-fits-all conversation. Happiness is unique and special to each of us. But whatever your happiness looks like, I want it for you.

ADVERSITY IS PART OF YOUR HAPPINESS

Over the course of this book, we have discussed the top career killers, as well as those steps we can all take to work toward building a successful career. During your journey, don't forget that adversity is part of your happiness. You will encounter bumps and obstacles, but you are going to have to face them, handle them, and eventually overcome them. For every person who has reached a great level of success, he or she can likely point to a large amount of adversity along the way. It is simply part of the adventure.

Far too many young men and women feel as if a dream career is their destiny. But the truth is that it takes hard work, a positive attitude, strategic and smart decisions, and a willingness to grit up and overcome all that clutters your path. Don't succumb to the adversity or the challenges, and certainly don't give up.

IF YOU BUILD IT, HE WILL COME

We have all heard this famous movie quote, "If you build it, he will come," from *Field of Dreams.* The same is true with your career: You will find endless opportunities if you create something special. We all want something really big right now. It takes time and effort to build a professional life of which you are proud.

- *You might find yourself in your second or third job in a short time . . . but that's okay.*
- *You might feel as if you are still "figuring it out," while your friends are humming along . . . but that's okay.*
- *You might feel like you are just never going to advance or move up in your career . . . but that's okay.*
- *You might feel like you should go back to school and study something new . . . but that's okay.*
- *You might feel like you need a change of location or even profession . . . but that's okay.*

Each of these potential challenges is not only normal but expected during your job journey. You just have to remember to keep stacking bricks and build your career. Eventually, you will find that all your trials, tribulations, and experiences add up to something extraordinary. It won't happen by chance. It will happen because of your purposeful decisions and willingness to keep moving one foot in front of the other.

GET UNSTUCK

At least once in your professional life you will find yourself stuck. Even if you avoid our five career killers and implement our five career builders, you might still end up stuck and unsure of where to go and what to do. If that happens, consider this list to help you get unstuck:

1. *Make a change.* A different job, a different career, or even going back to school may be in order. Sometimes the best way to get unstuck is to really just shake it up.
2. *Talk, Talk, Talk.* It is amazing how many problems are solved by simple communication. Talk with your family, with your friends, and with your colleagues to determine how you can reconnect and make a shift.
3. *Change Your Attitude.* Oftentimes, perspective is reality. Change your attitude to be more positive, welcoming, and excited about your life.
4. *Focus on Your Personal Life.* Many times, young men and women are unhappy in their workplace because of problems at home. A failing marriage, difficult children, or financial problems can all easily bleed into your professional life.
5. *Take a Vacation.* Just get away. Disconnect from your job, and refresh yourself.
6. *Relax.* Sometimes you just need to take a little time for yourself. A massage, a long lunch outdoors, or a good run may be the cure. It is amazing just how much a little time off can accomplish.
7. *See a Professional.* Therapists, psychiatrists, and life coaches are all great options to help you work through your struggles and get unstuck.

8. *Quit Your Job.* This seems like a pretty substantial reaction, but sometimes you just have to make a change. Quit your job before you fall into the practice of subpar performance.

9. *Use Your Resources.* The Internet, magazines, and this book can help you get unstuck. There is much to read and to learn. Use the vast resources available to you.

10. *Stick It Out.* Sometimes you just need to overcome an immediate obstacle or issue to get unstuck. Be patient, work through immediate obstacles, and see if you can reroute and keep going forward.

At the end of the day, you write the final chapter of your life with the choices you make, the people you spend time with, and your attitude as you approach and enjoy your life. Opportunities always come dressed in challenges and hard work. Make the most of them. Jim Rohn helps us round out this book by stating, "Success is nothing more than a few simple disciplines, practiced every day."

Career Killers/Career Builders has hopefully outlined extremely valuable and helpful steps that you can implement every day. Keep these suggestions at the top of your mind and think of them as you navigate each day of your professional life.

You will find that many of these suggestions will extensively help you throughout your personal life too. As much as many people feel their personal and professional lives are indeed separate entities, they are intimately connected, and turbulence in one can cause a bumpy ride in the other. All I want for you is happiness. I want you to realize endless success. I want you to awake each day, just like I do, and get fired up about going to work and completing your daily mission. When it comes down to it, you deserve it all.

Your life *does* count.

CPSIA information can be obtained
at www.ICGtesting.com
Printed in the USA
LVOW13s1804170517
534418LV00010B/38/P